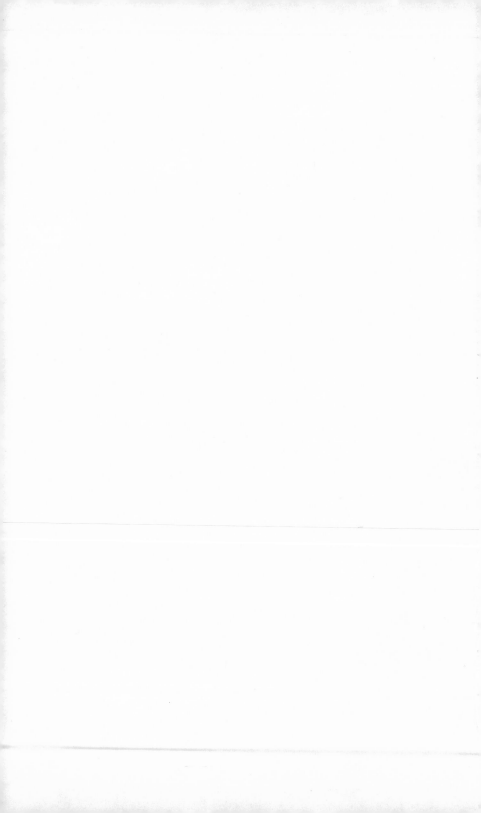

Sons of Baseball

Sons of Baseball

Growing Up with a Major League Dad

MARK BRAFF

ROWMAN & LITTLEFIELD
Lanham • Boulder • New York • London

Published by Rowman & Littlefield
An imprint of The Rowman & Littlefield Publishing Group, Inc.
4501 Forbes Boulevard, Suite 200, Lanham, Maryland 20706
www.rowman.com

86-90 Paul Street, London EC2A 4NE, United Kingdom

British Library Cataloguing in Publication Information Available

Library of Congress Cataloging-in-Publication Data

Names: Braff, Mark, 1955– author.
Title: Sons of baseball : growing up with a Major League dad ; foreword by
  Cal Ripken Jr. / Mark Braff.
Description: Lanham, Maryland : Rowman & Littlefield, [2023] | Includes
  bibliographical references. | Summary: "Sons of Baseball is full of
  personal stories from sons of major league baseball players who talk
  about what it was like growing up with a famous father. Along the way,
  we get a rare glimpse of the ballplayers themselves, not as pitchers,
  hitters, managers, and coaches, but as dads and granddads"—Provided by
  publisher.
Identifiers: LCCN 2022041138 (print) | LCCN 2022041139 (ebook) | ISBN
  9781538176887 (cloth) | ISBN 9781538176894 (epub)
Subjects: LCSH: Baseball players—United States—Biography. | Baseball
  players—Family relationships—United States. | Fathers and sons—United
  States—Biography.
Classification: LCC GV865.A1 B6457 2023 (print) | LCC GV865.A1 (ebook) |
  DDC 796.3570922 [B]—dc22/eng/20220901
LC record available at https://lccn.loc.gov/2022041138

To my father, who showed me how to be a dad

Contents

Foreword

CAL RIPKEN JR.

Growing up in a baseball family was fun, challenging, unique, and certainly never dull. I wouldn't trade it for the world.

My three siblings and I grew up in and around the game of baseball, and my brother Bill and I were fortunate enough to ultimately play at the highest level for a pretty long stretch. Most baseball fans know about Bill and me and our careers, but our sister, Elly, was a fantastic athlete and a terrific softball player, and our brother, Fred, excelled at soccer, a sport that we all played and enjoyed. Dad always encouraged us to play other sports to stay in shape while honing other skills.

Our love of baseball began when we were kids traveling across the country with Mom to meet up with Dad, who was managing minor league baseball all across the country. Cal Sr.'s career took him (and us) from Wisconsin to Washington, Miami to Elmira, Rochester to Dallas and Asheville. We logged a lot of miles, and the stories from the road might be even more interesting than the stories from the ballparks.

Growing up around baseball felt very normal and natural to us, and most of the time it was a blast. Most people think that Dad was heavily involved in our youth baseball games and practices, but the reality is that he was on the road coaching, and it was Mom who got us to our games, watched us play, and cheered us on.

Everyone knew Dad as "the encyclopedia of baseball," and he was certainly a wealth of knowledge, but Mom was the one who was with us most summers when we were just starting to play organized ball.

We definitely had an advantage having Dad to teach us the fundamentals and the right way to play the game, but he never stood over us or demanded we practice. He and Mom simply encouraged us to pursue what made us happy and helped when and where they could. It helped us develop our own love and passion for the game.

When they were at our games, they always did a great job of depressurizing the situation. They would sit and watch from way down the line, and we would rarely talk about the game right after it ended; rather, Dad would wait until the next day and gently offer some feedback on what he saw and how we might be able to practice and improve.

Dad loved saying "practice doesn't make perfect, perfect practice makes perfect" and "if it is worth doing, it is worth doing right." These lessons resonated with us and helped me when it was time for me to help my kids grow in sports.

Mom played a big role in this as well. As a kid, I had a terrible temper, and after a game, if I didn't play well or we suffered a tough loss, I would be so angry. She would tell me that being mad and upset wasn't a bad thing, but I should use that energy in a productive way—go for a run or do some pushups. It really helped me mature and understand how to control my negative emotions as a kid.

As I started to develop as a ballplayer, I started thinking about the prospect of actually playing baseball professionally. I had a huge growth spurt after my sophomore year in high school and really started to gain power and strength. I was a pitcher and a shortstop in high school. I started as a second baseman because before the growth spurt I couldn't make the throw from third or short! I knew many teams were thinking about drafting me as a pitcher, but even way back then I was hoping to be drafted as an everyday player. I couldn't imagine just playing once every five days.

When the Baltimore Orioles, my hometown team, which my dad coached for, drafted me in the second round, I was so excited. It was a dream come true.

I started my pro career in Bluefield, West Virginia, and I quickly realized that everyone who played professionally was pretty darn good and that every level would present a whole new set of challenges. At Bluefield, the Orioles had a shortstop named Bob Bonner, who came out of college. He was making plays that had me thinking I would never make it. After some helpful discussions with Dad, I started to make gains and continued to improve and move up the ladder.

I really started to think that the big leagues could be a possibility when I played in Charlotte, North Carolina, where I made the All-Star team, and we won the Southern League Championship. The next spring, I attended spring training with the Orioles and ended up at Triple-A Rochester, where I played most of the season and even played in the longest game in history, thirty-three innings!

August 7, 1981, was the day I was called up to the big leagues. Dad was a coach with the team, and Earl Weaver was the manager. It was a dream come true. Even better, a few years later I played with my brother Bill, and Dad was the manager! It was one of those things that we knew was special at the time, but I always wished we embraced it a little more when it was happening. Bill and I had our dad around, so we could ask him questions and rely on him in a special way, and we had each other for support and friendship throughout the season.

One funny thing that came out of having my dad in the same locker room was when I made the mistake of actually calling him "Dad" in front of my teammates. Man, I took some heat for that, and I made sure it didn't happen again.

There are also the rare times when being in a baseball family makes things more challenging. When dad was fired as Orioles manager, it hit us hard, and we were angry. We believed (and still do) that he didn't get the opportunity that he deserved. It took us some time to come to grips with the situation. Ultimately, I knew that I wanted to continue to play for my hometown team, but those were difficult days.

Dad didn't return to an Orioles game after that until the night of September 6, 1995, when I played in my 2,131st consecutive game. When the game was halted for a celebration in the middle of the fifth inning as it became official, I looked up to the suite where mom and dad were watching, and he and I locked eyes. A million words were shared without a word being spoken. It capsulized our lifetime through the game of baseball.

That's a glimpse into my story. I think you will enjoy reading the personal accounts of growing up in the world of baseball that eighteen of my fellow sons of professional players, managers, and coaches tell on the following pages. For each of us, it certainly was a unique childhood. Welcome to our world!

Acknowledgments

The existence of this book is tangible proof of the power of networking, as I did not know a single "son of baseball" when I began the project in January 2021. And so, challenge number one was to figure out how—or even if—I could connect with the people whose stories are collected in this book.

I began by sending a dozen or so emails to people I thought might (emphasis on "might") know a son of baseball (not likely) or someone who could connect me with someone who knows a baseball son (maybe).

The first person to respond favorably was David Newman, executive vice president and chief marketing, content, and communications officer for the New York Mets. David and I met many years ago (full disclosure: it's been a few decades) when we were both wet-behind-the-ears public relations guys; David for MSG Network and me for USA Network.

David introduced me to Jay Horwitz, a legend in the field of sports PR who for thirty-four years was the Mets' head of media relations and now serves the organization as vice president of Alumni Relations and team historian. An author himself (*Mr. Met: How a Sports-Mad Kid from New Jersey Became Like Family to Generations of Big Leaguers*), Jay was incredibly kind to this first-time writer and got the ball rolling by facilitating an introduction to Gil Hodges Jr.

Gil, in turn, introduced me to his good friend, Larry Berra, who became interview number two.

Vada Pinson III was interview number three. I found Vada on my own, having read some of his posts on a baseball necrology website and then tracking him down via LinkedIn.

Vada introduced me to his friend, Leo Cardenas Jr., who became interview number four.

Interview subject number five was Larry Doby Jr. I had read a story on Doby written by Zack Meisel, a writer for *The Athletic*. I reached out to Zack, who introduced me to Curtis Danburg, vice president of Communications and Community Impact for the Cleveland Guardians. Curtis graciously introduced me to Larry, despite the fact that my first email to Curtis began, "Hi Chris."

The sixth interview was conducted with Jerry Hairston Jr. I was introduced to Jerry by Jon Chapper, who at the time was assistant director of Public Relations for the Los Angeles Dodgers. I found Jon's contact info in the *Baseball America 2021 Directory*.

Next up was Michael Bouton. When I began this book project, I decided to keep it mostly on the down-low because I didn't know if it would ever see the light of day. Soon after, though, I remembered that the key to networking is to tell as many people as possible because one never knows who might have a valuable contact. This was proven true when I mentioned the book to my next-door neighbor, friend, and fellow baseball nut, Bob Berman. Bob told me he knew a guy who knew Michael Bouton. That guy was Peter Dykstra, who knows Michael from their work on environmental causes. Peter made the introduction.

Interview number eight was Matt Aker. The introduction was made by Marty Appel, a former New York Yankees PR guy who has authored more than twenty books, including *Pinstripe Empire: The New York Yankees from Before the Babe to After the Boss*. I knew of Marty but had only met him once—very briefly—thirty-plus years ago. Marty was kind enough to post a note about this project on his private Facebook group for families of former Yankee players, and Matt Aker reached out to me as a result.

Interview number nine was with Andy Hargrove, to whom I was introduced by the aforementioned Curtis (a.k.a. Chris) Danburg. I should take a moment here to also recognize the efforts of Andy's mom/Mike's wife, Sharon Hargrove, who went above and beyond to get me photos of Andy and Mike.

The tenth interview was with John W. Powell Jr. Using the *Baseball America 2021 Directory*, I reached out to Bill Stetka, director of Orioles Alumni, who put me in touch with John.

Next came Kevin Maris. Using the aforementioned directory, I contacted Michael Margolis, senior director of Communications and Media Relations for the Yankees. Michael introduced me to Gregory King, senior associate director of Marketing for the team. Gregory made the intro to Kevin.

Following Kevin were three more sons of former Yankee greats: Robby Richardson, Brandon Guidry, and Jafet Rivera.

The Richardson introduction was facilitated by Michael Bouton, which means that two chapters of this book were the result of my mentioning the project to my neighbor Bob.

The Guidry introduction was made by Gregory King, and the Rivera interview came via Ben Zettler, a digital marketing and e-commerce consultant who previously worked for five years at Steiner Sports. I was introduced to Ben by yet another neighbor (an ex-neighbor, to be accurate), Richard Felton.

Tony Peña Jr. was next, via an introduction from Dina Blevins, director of Community Investments/Alumni for the Kansas City Royals. I found Dina through the *Baseball America* directory.

Interview number sixteen was with Jeff McNally, to whom I was introduced by John W. Powell Jr. The two have known each other since they were kids when their dads starred for the Orioles.

Next was Dusty Wathan, with an intro from Dina Blevins, who happens to be Dusty's sister.

The final interview, with David Rodriguez, caps off not only the networking process but also the whole "you never know who might know someone" element. My wife, Laura, worked for many years at a senior community, Five Star Premier Residences, before retiring in April 2021. During that summer, she stopped in at Five Star to have lunch with some of her former colleagues. When the subject arose of what she and I are doing in retirement, she mentioned that I was working on this book. That led one of her former coworkers to say that her godson's father was a former major league baseball player. Thank you, Noemi Abreu, for volunteering that valuable piece of information and introducing me to David.

A big thank-you as well to Cal Ripken Jr. for contributing the foreword to this book, and to his public relations rep, John Maroon of Maroon PR, for making it happen.

I owe a deep debt of gratitude to all those mentioned above, both the interview facilitators and the interviewees. It goes without saying that this book would not exist without their help and generosity.

Other people kindly attempted to connect me with possible interview subjects, publishers, and literary agents, but, through no fault of their own, the leads resulted in dead ends. The outcome in no way diminishes my appreciation for their willingness to help me, and I would like to thank them all. This group includes Brad Adgate, Colleen Braff, Joe Billetdeaux, Mike Daniels, Mark Feinsand, Allan Goldstein, Rand Hoyt, Tyler Kepner, Richard Lynn, my sister Sari Reid, and Richard Zackon.

I would like to thank other family and friends, whose interest in the project helped me believe it had merit and that I could actually complete it.

In the latter group are my golf buddies Keith Edson, Mark Goldstein, and his son, Scott, and two other longtime friends, Jan Goldenberg and Steve Kaplan. If we were to take all the hours we've spent talking baseball over the years and apply them to more important pursuits, we probably could have solved most of the world's problems by now.

And, of course, my immediate family, whose love and support continually add rich new chapters to my life: My wife, Laura, who provided encouragement every step of the way and cheerfully helped proofread this book despite not being the least bit of a baseball fan; my son Gregg, his wife, Kelly, and their two daughters, Sarah and Emily; my son Jason, his wife, Colleen, their daughter, Charlotte, and son, Grant. Thank you all for always being there.

An enormous thank-you as well to my literary agent, Jill Marr, who believed in this project from the day I first reached out to her and who championed it every step of the way. And an equally heartfelt thank-you to my editor at Rowman & Littlefield, Christen Karniski. She and her team took this book up a level and patiently guided this first-time author through the publishing process.

I am also greatly appreciative of the "Free Advice Fridays" webinars run by Keri Barnum of New Shelves Books. Keri's tremendous insights into the publishing business were a big help to me and made me realize how naive I was when I embarked on this project. (Turns out, the process of authoring a book is pretty damn complex!)

We all go through life and compile mental snapshots of meaningful moments. The settings for so many of mine are from the stands at Yankee Stadium, where I have been fortunate to share so many thrills and great moments with my sons. These experiences, as well as similar ones with my father over the years, give me a very personal and meaningful understanding of the father-son connection through baseball.

While this book's dedication is to my father, I would like to take a moment to thank my late mother, Phyllis Braff, who loved me unconditionally and who instilled in me her love for reading. If she hadn't raised me to be a reader of books, I seriously doubt that I ever would have been a writer of one.

And of my dad, Milton Braff: He taught me so many things in life, including the mantra, "If you're going to do a job, do it right." I hope I did this one right, Dad.

Introduction

One of my fondest boyhood memories is that of tossing a baseball back and forth with my father. In my neck of the woods, New Jersey, this is called "having a catch." In some other environs, it's called "playing catch," which I must admit makes a lot more sense since you wouldn't, for example, call singing a duet "having a duet."

Regardless of verbiage, it has occurred to me over the years that the act of a father and son tossing a baseball back and forth often embeds itself in the memories of both parties, but particularly the son's, because it was a time when you had your dad all to yourself.

For me, it meant being out on the street in front of our house (a pretty quiet street, thankfully) on a warm summer night and throwing around an old baseball with my dad. He reminded me a bit of late-career Mickey Mantle because, like The Mick, it looked like every throw by my dad was adding a bit more wear and tear to an already aching shoulder. But he kept right on throwing.

Over the years, I have come to appreciate baseball's role as a connective tissue between fathers and sons; daughters, too, of course, but for purposes of this book, I am just considering the father-son connection.

I think the first time I ever thought about this was when I was watching a sitcom many years ago and one of the younger characters mentioned that, no matter how large the generation gap with his father, the one thing they could always talk about was baseball. Years later, *Field of Dreams*, one of the most popular baseball-centric films ever made, captured the essence of the baseball bond when Kevin Costner's character, Ray Kinsella, is briefly reunited with his deceased father, John (played by Dwier Brown), and asks him, for one last time, "Hey, Dad, wanna have a catch?"

I refer to *Field of Dreams* as a "baseball-centric" film because it really wasn't about baseball. It was about a father and his son, and how they were reunited through baseball; specifically, the act of playing catch.

As I thought about baseball as a father-son bonding experience in recent years, I began to wonder what it must be like when the dad is a major league baseball player. Is he happy to toss the ball around the yard with his son, or is asking your dad to have a catch the equivalent of an accountant's son asking his pop to add columns of numbers just for fun?

What's it like to be without your dad around the house for long stretches of time during the summer, the very same time when you're off from school and have all the time in the world to toss around a baseball?

How does it feel to be out with your dad only to find that you must share him with an autograph-seeking public?

And what about playing Little League? The self-esteem of so many young boys is tied to how good they are at sports. So, what happens when all the other kids and their parents know that you are the son of a major leaguer, and maybe you start hearing their voices, hushed perhaps but loud enough for you to hear, that you'll never be a professional baseball player like your dad?

For that matter, how does it feel when your dad goes 0 for 4 and strikes out twice with the bases loaded and you hear kids at school the next day saying he stinks? His failures are out there for the world to see. Your classmates don't discuss, and thousands of people don't boo, the aforementioned accountant when he makes a math error.

Is there pressure to go into "the family business"? Or, is it best to not even try, so as not to be held up to an absurdly high standard? Major league baseball players are, after all, the crème de la crème, a very select group that at any given time numbers less than eight hundred people on the entire planet.

What's it like having baseball stars—your dad's friends and "uncles" to you—hanging out at your home on a regular basis?

In writing this book, I sought answers to these questions and more from the only people who can address them—the sons of former major league baseball players. In the following pages, these "sons of baseball" talk about the challenges and rewards of growing up with fathers whose athletic talent enabled them to reach the pinnacle of their profession.

The men interviewed for this book are true sons of baseball, not only because they were raised in part by professional baseball players, but also because, in the broader sense, many of them were raised by the game itself. They grew up immersed in the distinct sounds and aromas of baseball. The locker rooms, cinder block-lined corridors beneath the stands, dugouts, and fields were the playgrounds and landscapes of their youth. On the following pages, they tell their stories, and along the way, we get a rare glimpse of the players not as pitchers, hitters, managers, and coaches, but as dads.

Jerry Hairston and Jerry Hairston Jr.

Following Grandpa and Dad into the Family Business

In the long history of major league baseball, there are only five families who boast three generations of players: the Bells (Gus, David, and Buddy), the Boones (Ray, Bob, Bret/Aaron), the Colemans (Joe, Joe Jr., and Casey), the Schofield/Werths (Dick, Dick, and Jayson) and the Hairstons (Sam, Jerry/John, Jerry Jr./Scott).

The Hairston's baseball family tree is quite remarkable. It begins with Sam Hairston, who played seven seasons in the Negro Leagues before getting a four-game cup of coffee with the Chicago White Sox in 1951. Sam's son, John, played in three games for the Chicago Cubs in 1969, appearing as the first Black catcher in the team's history. Another of Sam's sons, Jerry, played fourteen years in the major leagues from 1973 to 1989, and a third son, Sam Jr., played in the minor leagues. Two of John's sons, Jason and John Jr., played in the minor leagues. Two of Jerry's sons played in the major leagues. They are Scott, who played from 2004 to 2014, and Jerry Jr., whose big league career spanned 1998–2013.

If you followed that without rereading, you might qualify for a career in genealogy.

During Jerry Sr.'s fourteen-year major league career, he played all but part of one season with the White Sox (a mid-career pit stop with the Pittsburgh Pirates). But he also played for three years in the Mexican League, from 1978 to 1980, when it appeared his major league career was over, only to be "rediscovered" by the White Sox for a nine-season run starting in 1981.

The Birmingham, Alabama, native was the third-round draft pick of the White Sox in 1970 and made his major league debut on July 26, 1973. Defensively, he was primarily an outfielder, seeing significant time at all three positions, along with some time at first base and a single game at second base. He led the American League in pinch hits for three straight seasons starting in 1983, and still holds the White Sox career record with eighty-seven. Perhaps his most notable was a two-out single up the middle against Milt Wilcox of the Detroit Tigers in April 1983, a hit that broke up Wilcox's bid for a perfect game. Hairston Sr. was a contact hitter who walked more than he struck out (282/240) on his way to a career .258 batting average in just over two thousand plate appearances.

◆

Jerry Hairston Jr. was born May 29, 1976, in Des Moines, Iowa, during his father's fourth season with the White Sox. He grew up with two brothers—including Scott, another future major leaguer—and two sisters. And, of course, a baseball lineage that is almost hard to fathom.

"I was the oldest. I just wanted to be around my dad, and he just so happened to be a baseball player. And, you know, what kid at two, three, four, five years old doesn't want to throw a ball or swing the bat? I just loved having a bat in my hands. So, from a very young age, I fell in love with the sport, and I knew this is what I want to do. My dad obviously helped me. My grandfather encouraged me. It was nothing that was forced. It was just something that I always wanted to do."

Growing up around the game, it wasn't until he was "six, seven, or eight" years old that Jerry Jr. realized his dad did something unique for a living.

"I remember being at Payne Park in Sarasota and I got a chance to go to the stadium, the spring training facility, with my dad. And he was signing a lot of autographs, giving a lot of time. And I was being a baby. I wanted his time and attention. I started crying because that was my time with him. I think my dad was starting that day and decided to take the day off, just to deal with me. I was being a pain in the butt."

As time went by, Jerry Jr. realized that autograph signing came with the job and that it could have been worse.

"I was fortunate. My dad wasn't a superstar. It wasn't like he was recognized everywhere he went. It was never overwhelming. My dad always handled it well. He always treated the fans in a kind way."

Jerry Jr. spent his formative years in Arlington, Texas.

"My dad was playing in Mexico. My mom is Mexican. In fact, my first language was Spanish. I really didn't know a whole lot of English. Then [White Sox manager] Tony La Russa and [general manager] Roland Hemond came down to scout some pitching [during the major league players strike in 1981] and they saw my dad. They're like, 'Wow, you're still playing?' And after the strike was over, the White Sox signed my dad. That was a life-changing thing for our family. You know, my dad was almost done. He was thinking about hanging it up because, you know, he was down there raking in the Mexican League, winter and summer, and he just wasn't getting another look. But him sticking with it and not giving up allowed him to play [many] more years in the big leagues. And, who knows, if he didn't have that opportunity, where I would be as far as a baseball player, and Scott too. So, that definitely changed our life course, my father not giving up."

Mom, of course, played a big role in raising Jerry Jr. and his siblings.

"My mother obviously was the anchor of our family because my dad traveled. But they did an incredible job keeping the family together. They worked extremely well together. They're still married.

You know, being a big leaguer is taxing on you. It can obviously tax a family, too. So, for them to stay together, it's definitely a testament to them."

Even during the winter, "it was still Mom's house."

"But it was always good to have my dad home in the winter. He helped shovel snow, and it was always cool to have him around."

Dad would often have his baseball buddies over the house.

"I remember guys like Chet Lemon, Lou Whitaker, they'd come over to the house with their families. I remember he invited some of the Negro League players that knew my grandpa. That was always a great time. [Guys like] Ted 'Double Duty' Radcliffe. Funny dude. I remember that for African American History Month, I was in the seventh or eighth grade, and one of the kids in my class did a whole biography on Double Duty Radcliffe. I was like, 'Dude, he was just at my house four months ago!' It was definitely kind of a cool experience to see that, and just to know that these guys, even though they were iconic figures, they were still ordinary men."

Jerry Jr. would often accompany his dad to the ballpark and loved playing on the field after the games—but only if the Sox won that day.

"During day games, once the White Sox were done at Comiskey Park, if they won, we'd go run out on the field and play for a little bit. So, we were always hoping that the White Sox would win. And then we'd go out there for about twenty, thirty minutes after the game and play on the field. That was always a treat."

But why only if the White Sox won?

"Out of respect. Carlton Fisk's son, Casey, we'd always go out there. I learned at a young age that winning is important. You know, you don't get paid just to show up, you get paid to win, so I knew that was important at a young age. So, it [playing on the field after the game] was a reward. And if you lose, you don't get rewarded, and rightfully so."

Jerry Jr.'s baseball education extended beyond the field as well.

"I loved sitting down and watching the games with my dad during the postseason. He'd point out certain things and I would learn a lot by watching the game and hearing my dad talk. I loved even when my dad was playing on TV. I could just sit there, watch the game, and learn from Ken 'Hawk' Harrelson and Don Drysdale, who were the broadcasters back then, and just hearing guys that have played the game talk about the game. I had to make sure I had my homework done so I was ready to go at seven o'clock to watch the White Sox play."

The advice his dad imparted was about more than just baseball.

"[He said], 'You know, the most important thing is just being a good person, a good citizen. The baseball stuff is just gravy. If you become a baseball player, great. If not, the most important thing is that you become a productive member of society.' He always gave me confidence. I think that sometimes sons, they look up to their fathers but feel that's the ceiling, and then it's almost like subconsciously you don't want to be better than your father. And some of these sons don't make it to the big leagues because of that. My dad always told me at a young age, 'Don't be me. Be better than me.' It's something I talked to Clay Bellinger, Cody Bellinger's dad, about. I played against Clay, and he said he always instilled in his son, 'Be better than me.' And that obviously helped because Cody's a better player than his old man [laughs]."

Jerry Jr. was drafted out of high school by the Baltimore Orioles in 1995 but did not sign, choosing instead to attend Southern Illinois University. He was drafted again by the Orioles, in 1997, and signed his first pro contract. He made his major league debut in 1998, a triumphant moment made bittersweet by the passing of his grandfather, Sam, in October 1997.

"I was definitely disappointed [about that]. But he saw me get drafted. In fact, he and my dad went down to Birmingham to work me out. My grandfather worked me out. He said, 'Hey, let me see Jerry, let me put my eyes on him.' And he worked me out and said,

'Hey, he's ready. He needs to sign.' Having the stamp of approval from both my dad and my grandfather, who would never lie to you, definitely gave me confidence. And when he passed, obviously it was a sad time for our family. I would have loved having him see me get to the big leagues, have a long career. It just didn't happen. But I like to think I did him proud with the career that I had, especially with the injuries that I had. You know, he was a better player than I was, but he didn't get the opportunity. That's why I played so hard."

Did not getting a shot at playing in the big leagues at a younger age leave his grandfather embittered?

Jerry Hairston Jr. with his grandfather Sam (left) and dad Jerry, three generations of major league ballplayers. *Jerry Hairston Jr.*

"He was never bitter. He had a cup of coffee [in the big leagues]. You know, they thought back then, 'We'll give him a cup of coffee, that'll keep his mouth shut.' He was a triple crown winner in the Negro Leagues before he signed with the White Sox. After his playing days, he was a scout. He signed some big leaguers, including my dad and Lamar Johnson, who had a long career. I remember running into [Hall of Fame relief pitcher] Goose Gossage. I believe it was in Denver while I was a player covering the World Series between the Red Sox and Rockies in '07. I ran into Gossage, and he had fond memories of my grandfather, just saying, 'I loved him.' So many people were impacted by my grandfather in this game. And that's something that I'm extremely proud of."

One wonders if the Hairstons' baseball success can be attributed to nature or nurture.

"I think it's both. You have to have the talent. But we all had a passion for the game. You have to have that love first. If you don't have that love, then you're not going to train hard when nobody's watching. You're not going to continue to pursue this game when you get knocked to the ground. Because this game will do it to you. You got to keep fighting, keep getting better. So, I think we all had that, you know, we just loved the game and had that passion, and we all encouraged each other."

Jerry Jr. recalls the thrill of getting the call to the big leagues.

"I was in AA in the Orioles organization, and Joe Ferguson, who was the catcher for the Dodgers when Hank Aaron broke Babe Ruth's [home run] record in Atlanta, he was my manager. He called me into his office and said, 'Hey, man, you had a great season. You're going to the big leagues. You got the call.' It was an incredible feeling, an incredible moment. We didn't have cell phones at the time, so I had to go call my dad and my family."

Was he surprised to make the jump from AA to the big leagues, skipping over AAA ball?

"Honestly, I really wasn't surprised because I was hitting around .330 in double-A. There were rumors that I might get called up. So, I wasn't surprised, but still, I mean, until it happens for sure, you don't know.

"My parents flew from Chicago to Baltimore. The next day, I got to the stadium and saw my name in the lineup. I was in the same lineup with [future Hall of Famer] Roberto Alomar. I played second base and Robbie's the greatest second baseman, in my opinion, who ever lived. He was DH'ing that day, and just to be in the same lineup as him and Rafael Palmeiro, Harold Baines, Cal Ripken Jr., it was humbling."

Jerry Jr. went on to carve out a sixteen-year major league career, during which he played every position except pitcher and catcher.

In 2009, Jerry Jr. and his brother, Scott, played for Mexico in the World Baseball Classic.

"That was the first time we ever played on the same team. I'm four years older than Scott, so we never got a chance to play Little League together or high school ball together. My mom is from Sonora, Mexico, so she was happy that we represented her homeland. And we were so happy to do that for her because my mom was the one that really kept our family together. She was always the foundation and was an incredible mother, making sure that we all went to our games and got our schoolwork done. And then getting the chance to play some exhibition games in Hermosillo, where my parents got married, was something special for her. I think it was the first game Scott and I played together. We both homered."

The following year, Jerry Jr. and Scott were teammates again, this time with the San Diego Padres.

"It was a great thing for our family. I signed with them and then a week or so later, the Padres traded for Scott. That was awesome. But Scott was banged up, man. He just could never get healthy that season. But, you know, it was still cool being on the same team with him. It was a great experience."

Of all the Hairstons, Jerry Jr. is the only one with a World Series ring as a player, having won a World Championship with the New York Yankees in 2009.

"I don't hang that over anybody. I felt I was very fortunate to be a part of that team. I was traded [to New York] mid-season. They needed a guy like me to play everywhere because they had everything as far as superstar talent. My brother didn't get a chance to play in a World Series. My dad never got a chance, and of course, my grandfather didn't. So, I kind of felt like it was all of us, you know? I represented everybody. I remember I was a little nervous when I got my first at-bat in the postseason. It was in the thirteenth inning. I was a little nervous, but I remembered my grandfather's blood, my dad's blood, runs through my veins, I'm not alone here. That's how I approached it."

Today, Jerry Jr. is a studio analyst for SportsNet LA. He has three children of his own, a boy and two girls. His parents live in Arizona.

"They're [outstanding] grandparents. My sisters have kids, my brother has kids, so they do a great job of helping all of us out. Their grandchildren love their *abuelita* [Spanish for grandmother] and their grandad. We get a chance to spend a lot of time with each other."

It's early, but it's not out of the realm of possibility that Jerry Jr.'s son, Jackson, might make the Hairstons a four-generation major league family. Jackson was fifteen years old when Jerry Jr. offered this scouting report:

"He's a really good player. He's got a passion for it. He works hard. He's a switch-hitter like his grandfather, and he has a way better swing than I did. He can run, play the infield, play the outfield. He definitely has a great foundation, and you never know what the future holds.

"And I tell him that he can do whatever he wants. He has a 4.3 GPA in high school and speaks extremely well. He could be a lawyer. He could be a doctor. He could be a broadcaster. A baseball player."

For those who might be wondering, Jerry Jr.'s son is not named after Hall of Famer Reggie Jackson.

"It was just a name that I happened to like. Ken Griffey Jr. was upset at me for naming him Jackson because he felt we should name him Jerry and then call him Trey. Ken Griffey Jr. has a son they call Trey. Jose Cruz Jr. has a son called Trey as well. But I wanted [my son] to be his own man. I wanted him to have his own name and then maybe in the future when he has a son, he can name him Jackson Jr."

But the Hairston name, well, that's something else entirely.

"The Hairston name, I think, is pretty much a respected name. Obviously, we're not the Griffeys or the Bondses; we didn't have that type of talent or ability, but, you know, we loved this game, and the game was good to us."

Roger Maris and Kevin Maris

Still Teaching Lessons from Dad

It's difficult to believe that a player who hit sixty-one home runs in a season to break a record set thirty-four years earlier by Babe Ruth, as Roger Maris did in 1961, could possibly be underrated, and yet the case could be made that Maris is exactly that.

When people think of Maris, they think of the "61 in '61." Casual baseball fans probably do not know much more than that about the left-handed slugger. But there was so much more to Maris than that record-setting season.

For starters, the Hibbing, Minnesota, native was voted the American League's Most Valuable Player in 1960, the year before his home run barrage (he won the award in 1961 as well), on the strength of a thirty-nine-home run, league-leading 112 RBI, .952 OPS season. He also won a Gold Glove award that year for his defensive prowess in right field for the Yankees.

Speaking of defense, it was that facet of Maris's game that quite possibly secured the Yankees' World Series win over the Giants in 1962. The Yankees led game seven, 1–0, in the bottom of the ninth. Matty Alou led off the inning with a bunt single. After Felipe Alou and Chuck Hiller struck out, Willie Mays doubled to right field. Maris retrieved the ball and made a great throw to hold Matty Alou—the tying run—on third base. Willie McCovey then lined out to end the game and give the Yankees their twentieth World Championship. The throw, as they say, was not the kind of thing that showed up in a box score, but it was emblematic of Maris's ability to influence a game in ways other than by hitting a home run.

In all, Maris was a seven-time all-star. He played in seven World Series (all in the decade of the 1960s) and hit six home runs in the Fall Classic.

He was signed by the Cleveland Indians organization out of high school, turning down a football scholarship to the University of Oklahoma. They likely were impressed by the four kickoffs he returned for touchdowns—in one game!

Maris made his major league debut with the Cleveland Indians in 1957, was traded to the Kansas City A's in June of the following year, and to the Yankees in the winter of 1959. The Yankees traded Maris to the St. Louis Cardinals before the 1967 season, and his winning pedigree and still well-rounded skill set helped the Cards to the World Series that season—a seven-game defeat of the Boston Red Sox—and again in 1968, when they lost in seven games to the Detroit Tigers. In the 1967 series, Maris batted .385 with ten hits.

Maris retired after the 1968 season at the age of thirty-three. His uniform number 9 was retired by the Yankees in 1984, bringing him full-circle from an estrangement with the organization that began with his trade to St. Louis and ended in 1978. The ill-will stemmed primarily from a wrist injury that Maris incurred during the 1965 season. The Yankees' medical staff and front office played down the extent of the injury and forced Maris to play hurt. His performance suffered, and he was portrayed as a malcontent by the press and booed by the fans. Maris and the team mended fences in time for him to participate in a championship flag-raising ceremony prior to the home opener in 1978. The reunion was sealed when team owner George Steinbrenner agreed to pay for new sod to be installed at the high school baseball field in Maris's hometown of Gainesville, Florida, a field now named after Maris.

After retirement, Maris and his brother, Rudy, ran an Anheuser-Busch beer distributorship in Gainesville. The former baseball star was diagnosed with lymphatic cancer in 1983 and died at the age of fifty-one in 1985. In 1999, a US postage stamp was released in his honor, and his legacy received renewed attention with the premiere of the film *61**, directed by Billy Crystal, in 2001. (The asterisk in the title refers to one that supposedly accompanied the notation in the baseball record book for the sixty-one home runs because Maris's season was 162 games as opposed to Ruth's 154; in fact, no such asterisk ever existed.)

◆

Kevin Maris was born in August 1960 as his father was in the midst of winning the first of his two American League Most Valuable Player awards. Kevin was the third of six children, four boys book-ended by two girls, born to Roger and Pat Maris.

"They [the girls] kept us in line," Kevin jokes.

The family lived in Kansas City, Missouri, until Roger retired after the 1968 season, at which time they relocated to Gainesville, Florida.

"When Dad was traded to the Kansas City Athletics, Dad thought he was going to be there for quite a while. He built a nice house and, as little kids, there were a bunch of us running around. We had an upstairs room where we could do anything. We could roller skate. It was a great playroom to be able to grow up in and have fun in it."

But it wasn't always easy, what with his dad traveling so much of the year.

"We missed him for about eight months out of the year. I think that bothered him a lot, that he wasn't there more because of his job, but we understood it. Was it hard on us at times? I'm sure it was to a point, but whenever he was home, we always cherished every minute we had with him. He appreciated just playing and hanging out with us and screwing around in the backyard, playing different games. We played all kinds of card games, and he had a lot of fun doing that with us.

"When he got traded to the Cardinals [from the Yankees], it was a real big plus for us. I was seven or eight years old, and we'd go to the ballpark with him and hang out and play on the field, go into the dugout, the locker room. For a kid seven or eight, it was just a dream come true. Just to be around those guys and listen to their stories so up close was a real treat for us as young kids.

"One of the great experiences was the father-son game that they'd always have. We always had a great time doing that. We'd all dress up in Dad's uniform and we played a game. It was an experience that you can only dream about, and we were fortunate enough to be able to live it."

Sometimes, his dad's work buddies would drop by the house.

"Mickey [Mantle] would come by from time to time. Whitey Herzog [former Cardinals and Kansas City Royals manager] would come by all the time. We grew up about a mile from Whitey in Kansas City when he was there, and we got to be good friends with him. The Shannons [Cardinals third baseman Mike Shannon and his family] and Bob Allison [a former major league outfielder] would come by.

"I don't think we were star struck because, you know, like Mickey, we grew up with him and his boys, so they were just part of the family. We wouldn't say so-and-so is coming over because Dad was reserved about it."

Roger Maris was a World Series fixture in the 1960s, playing in the Fall Classic every year except 1965 and 1966, and in 1969 when he was already retired.

"When Dad did things, he was always a champion at whatever he did. I mean, he'd go off to different events, like golf tournaments or hunting events or whatever, and he'd come back with a first- or second-place trophy. I remember he went to a governor's goose hunt one year, and he shot the biggest goose. He just loved to compete."

Despite Maris's winning pedigree, some Cardinals were skeptical when he was traded to St. Louis by the Yankees.

"When he first came to the Cardinals, they were just kind of skeptical of how he was going to be, whether he was going to be a big shot or whatever. And during the first couple of days in spring training, he hit a ball in the gap or something. And he turned it into a double, going in there and sliding hard. And that kind of set the tone that he was there to win and compete. That's the way Dad was. He was not there to mess around, he's there to win, whatever it took to win a game, whether it's a ground ball to second base or to lay down a bunt, he was about winning."

Kevin started playing in organized baseball leagues at the age of ten, when the family was living in Gainesville.

"He was always there whenever we wanted to practice or work out. He wasn't a guy that was going to force it on you. If you wanted to play, great, if you didn't want to play, he understood that. I remember a time that I was like ten years old playing in a ten- to twelve-year-old league. And there was a kid who came up to the plate at the end of the game, had the bases loaded, and I guess he struck out or whatever. So, I got in the car and made a dumb comment like, 'I'm glad I didn't strike out,' or whatever. Dad stopped the car and turned around, and he said, 'Don't ever let me hear you say that. If you're going to compete in sports, you got to love and thrive being in those positions.' And from that point on, I always looked at it as you need to be in that position. The way he put it was no matter how big the situation, you're going to have success and there's a lot of times you're going to fail, but at the end of the day you just gotta go out there and give it your best shot, and that's why you play the sport. That was a big moment for me."

Kevin didn't play high school baseball until his junior year at Oak Hall, when he was seventeen.

"For some reason, the school didn't have a field, but by my junior year, we had a lot of players who wanted to play. And so, Dad said,

'Well, why don't we build a field?' We got together in 1977 and built a field. He was out there, helped design it, and laid the sod."

The sod was courtesy of Yankee owner George Steinbrenner.

"Dad was a little skeptical about going back [to Yankee Stadium]. If it wasn't for George, I'm not sure my dad would have gone back. Mr. Steinbrenner was always good to us and treated Dad very well. He promised Dad that he would donate the sod. And so, we ended up putting the sod on the field and it was pristine, and now it's named after Dad."

The Roger Maris–Yankees relationship was something that he sometimes discussed with Kevin.

"He enjoyed playing in New York. He thought New York was one of the greatest places to play, especially when you're on your game, and Dad was on his game for quite a few years with the Yankees. It got tough toward the end. It was mainly the media stirring things up, and he had to deal with that. He didn't care for the attention he received. He just liked doing his job. The media and the limelight stuff, that wasn't his cup of tea; it's just something that he had to learn to deal with. He wasn't that guy who wanted to be the center of attention.

"He ended up breaking his hand in early '65. He slid into home, and he jammed his fingers into the umpire's shoe, and that's what ended up breaking his hand. And they [the team's medical staff] told him it wasn't broken. And they made him play that year. I remember as the years went on that he really had to grind his fingers out to get them straightened out in the morning. He had surgery after the '65 season, and it kind of took a little bit of pop away from him. He had to become a little different hitter, which he wasn't too happy about doing. He was going to retire in '66, but they traded him to the Cardinals, and history kind of wrote itself there."

When he finally returned to Yankee Stadium in 1978, Maris received a rousing welcome from the packed house on opening day.

"He probably had a little reluctancy of how he was going to be received, and when they gave him the ovation it was warming to him that they welcomed him back. That meant a lot to him at the time."

Around that time, Kevin graduated from high school and took time off to work as an assistant golf pro at the Marco Island golf course in Florida.

"I did that for about a year and then I decided I probably should go back to school. Santa Fe Community College had just started their baseball program, so I went out, made the team, and played that year with them. And then I signed as a free agent with the Cardinals the following year to give baseball a shot."

Kevin quickly learned what it meant to be the son of a former baseball star.

"The first article I got in pro ball was, 'This Maris No Threat to Ruth' [laughs]. And I'm like, why would I expect to be my dad? No one else in the game has done what my dad has done. If I did half of what he did, I'd be more than satisfied. But it was tough at times because everyone always expected so much, you know? But I wasn't caught up in being that. I appreciated who my dad was. I think a lot of kids in my situation that have famous fathers that are sports figures or celebrities, they try to distance themselves from their parents or father, mother, whoever it is. I think they make it hard on themselves from a mental standpoint, as opposed to just appreciating who you are. If you want to call me Roger Maris's son, I couldn't care less. That's who I am. I'm going to be Roger Maris's son until I'm dead and gone, so why should I try to fight that the whole time?

"When I was playing pro ball, I had three guys every night who would sit up in the stands in the upper corner. And they were like, 'You suck! You're nothing like your dad.' And I was like, yeah, if I worried about that I'd have been in a mental institution a long time ago."

Kevin was a left-handed hitter like his dad, with the same sweet, fluid swing. There was just one problem.

"I didn't have the legs. I was gifted with my mom's legs, not my dad's [laughs]."

Kevin hurt his knee during sliding drills on his very first day in pro ball.

"I went to five different doctors, and they had five different opinions. At that time, all they had was the big knife and the scar on your knee for exploratory [surgery]. I said, I'm not going to have them cut it and have them say it's just a sprain. So, it got somewhat healthy, and I guess I was probably 70 percent healthy the rest of the year. I could still play and steal bases here and there, but it was never right.

Kevin Maris gets some pointers from his dad, Roger.
Kevin Maris

I'd played tournament golf prior to playing college baseball, so I went back to my golf because it [the knee] didn't affect me when I was playing golf. If I hadn't had my golf, I probably would have tried [baseball] a bit longer."

Following his first season of baseball, Kevin spent the winter working out with his dad.

"We'd work out a little bit in the weight room. He never lifted weights in his life. There was this overhead press. He goes, 'Well, how much should I put on there?' And I was like, 'Heck, I don't know, I'm just [starting] myself.' So, he put the pin on the bottom, and he goes [Kevin makes a lifting motion], 'How's that, is that good?' [laughs]. He had a natural strength. In the months we were working out, he had to stop because he started growing out of his shirts."

Sometimes, a sailor hat was his dad's dress mode.

"I remember that in New York he sometimes wore disguises walking the streets because he really couldn't walk the streets without people recognizing him. He had a little sailor-type hat on one time with glasses. It was funny. He had to do that because if he didn't, he'd draw a crowd and wouldn't get to do the things that he wanted to do with us."

To this day, more than half a century after Roger Maris played his final game, people come up to Kevin to talk about his dad.

"They get pretty tickled about it. What's interesting is that they're always talking about how good a ballplayer he was defensively. The people that saw him really know the kind of player he was, throwing runners out, taking the extra base, breaking up double plays . . . the little things. It's neat to hear them talk about that side of it."

In July 1984, less than eighteen months before his death, Roger Maris had his uniform number 9 retired by the Yankees.

"Retiring Dad's number was probably one of the greatest accomplishments that Dad was awarded. I mean, the best of the best played with the Yankees and for Dad to be in a group of the best speaks for itself. And to have him experience that before he passed away was very meaningful."

Today, Kevin coaches baseball at his old high school, and he founded and is still involved with the Florida Hardballers, a travel team for kids from ages eight to eighteen.

Kevin still imparts some of his dad's wisdom to young players, including:

"If you're going to do something, do it first-class or don't do it at all."

"Preparation and attention to detail of the smallest things are what prepares you for success."

"Pressure is listening to what other people expect of you. Just do what you do best and let the chips fall where they may."

"Understand failure. Learn from failure. Failure is your best teacher as long as you analyze the positives of your failures."

In addition to coaching teams, Kevin also runs an annual Kevin Maris Baseball Camp and is involved with the Roger Maris Celebrity Golf Tournament started by his father in the early 1980s.

"[Dad] was only able to come to one. He got sick for the second one and by the third one, he had passed. It's a tribute to all of his celebrity buddies that have come back over the years. It speaks volumes about what they thought of Dad as a person, to come back and help his family promote and raise funds for the Roger Maris Cancer Center."

The cancer center is in Fargo, North Dakota, where Roger Maris spent much of his youth and starred in scholastic sports. Fargo is also home to the Roger Maris Museum.

"People [tell us] they had family members who were treated at Roger Maris and, you know, that's a whole new legacy that Dad has become a part of."

Larry Doby and Larry Doby Jr.

From Baseball to Billy Joel

Larry Doby fell about three months short of becoming a household name. He debuted in the major leagues with the Cleveland Indians on July 5, 1947, at the age of twenty-three. He was the first African American player in the American League, but his landmark ascension to the big leagues was overshadowed at the time, and in the history books, by Jackie Robinson's debut with the National League's Brooklyn Dodgers that April, an event that is celebrated to this day as the official breaking of Major League Baseball's "color barrier."

That said, Doby's trailblazing was accomplished in the face of the same racial taunts and discrimination that Robinson famously endured. In certain respects, Doby's path was even more difficult considering he went directly from the Negro Leagues to the Major Leagues. He played in a doubleheader for the Newark Eagles on July 4, 1947, and the very next day he was in Cleveland, playing for the Indians. He did not have the benefit of participating in a couple of major league spring training camps and a season in the minor leagues, as Robinson did.

Still, Doby forged a major league career that earned him enshrinement into the Hall of Fame in 1998. He played the bulk of his career with Cleveland (1947–1955) and finished up with the Chicago White Sox and Detroit Tigers (1956–1959). He was a seven-time all-star and runner-up to Yogi Berra in the American League's Most Valuable Player voting in 1954. That fall, Doby became the first Black player to hit a home run in the World Series when he went deep against the New York Giants. He twice led the American League in home runs, including his MVP runner-up campaign in 1954 when he also led the league in runs batted in. He eclipsed the 100 RBI mark five times in his thirteen-year career.

Before joining Cleveland, Doby left behind a brief but impactful Negro League legacy. His Newark Eagles won the Negro League World Series in 1946, defeating Satchel Paige and the famed Kansas City Monarchs.

After his playing days, Doby coached for the Montreal Expos, the White Sox, and Indians. In 1978, he was named manager of the White Sox, once again finding himself second in the history books after another Robinson—Frank—became the major league's first African American manager in 1975.

In 1997, the Indians retired Doby's uniform number (14) on the fiftieth anniversary of his major league debut. A statue of Doby stands outside Cleveland's ballpark, at the corner of East Ninth Street and Larry Doby Way.

Doby was born in South Carolina and moved to Paterson, New Jersey, as a young boy after his father, David, drowned when he fell from a boat. In New Jersey, Doby lettered in four sports at Eastside High School. Throughout his life, Doby remained proud of his Paterson roots, and, in 1998, the city honored him with the dedication of Larry Doby Athletic Field at Eastside Park. In 2002, a statue of Doby was added to the facility.

In 2003, Doby died of cancer in Montclair, New Jersey, at the age of seventy-nine.

◆

Larry Doby Jr. was born in Paterson in 1957, near the end of his dad's playing career in the major leagues, and grew up in Montclair.

He was the middle child and the only boy among the five offspring of Larry and Helyn Doby, high school sweethearts who were married for fifty-eight years until Helyn's death in 2001.

"Our house was awesome. It was full of love. It was loud. My mom came from a family of ten children and my father was an only child. So, you know, not only did my mother give my dad a family, but she gave him an extended family. [For my parents], it was a love affair that started in high school. I'm sure their marriage wasn't perfect, but we never saw them fight or anything like that. In fact, the only argument I remember my parents having was when my father wanted to open a bar and my mother didn't think it was such a good idea.

"Fast-forward: He lost a whole lot of money. Should've listened to my mom."

How was it growing up with four sisters?

"Sisters are a trip, you know? They're in the bathroom all the time. They're dancing, they're playing music, they're on the phone. I love them all to death. I would have loved to have a brother, but I'm glad that I had my sisters. And I had a ton of cousins because my mother's family was ten and they were all basically in the vicinity.

"As a little boy, there were famous people in my house, which didn't mean anything to me, you know? Bill Russell, Willie Mays, Don Newcombe, Willie Naulls . . . all kinds of people like that. I can remember, you know, Willie Mays being in the house and I'm like, 'Oh yeah, Dad, cool. Can I go out and play?' And now I'm kicking myself, wishing I would have sat there and listened or asked questions. But, anyway, they were just Dad's friends."

Larry Jr. says his father never placed an emphasis on his celebrity.

"My father was so adamant on education and sports that I never got lost in the novelty or celebrity of it. You know, he was my dad and I never really saw him play. He was low-key and humble and very understated. And he was unknown to a large degree. And so, you get used to at a very early age of being fiercely proud of your dad, but also knowing that people don't know who he is. And growing up in Montclair and living in the same town as Yogi Berra, it's easy to be overshadowed, you know?"

The Doby and Berra families were friends with one another.

"I'm friends with Dale and Larry (two of Yogi Berra's sons) to this day and I knew Yogi and [his wife] Carmen all my life. Yogi, unlike some other people in baseball, was good to my father from day one. They had a long-standing friendship and did a lot of things together. Yogi's golf tournament, my father was always there. My high school, years after I was out, was trying to raise money. My father and Yogi signed autographs for free. They just had a tremendous amount of respect for each other, and love and friendship."

Having come of age after his dad's playing career was over, did Larry Jr. speak much about those days with his dad?

"He was one of those people, and I don't know to this day why, but he never really talked about [his playing days]. The only time I heard about it was when he was on the phone with a reporter or when he was on the phone with Mr. Newcombe because that was his guy, and they'd start cussing back and forth. The names that I heard in my house were the good guys. I didn't hear the names of the bad guys. So, if I heard a name in my house, I would learn to associate that this guy had something positive to do with my father. So, from the time I was a little kid, I heard Joe Gordon's name. I heard Jim Hegan's name. I heard Steve Gromek, Bob Lemon, and so forth. There are so many things that I would love to have asked him and my mother that, when they're here, you really don't think of."

Larry Sr.'s reticence in talking about his career was not due to a lack of interest on his son's part.

"At some point when you were a little kid, I'm sure you said, 'Hey Dad, what do you do? Where do you go for eight hours a day?' Well, I had that same curiosity, and the answer was, 'I don't talk about that. That was yesterday. I deal with today and the future. And if you want to learn about it, look it up in the history books.' And I'm like, that's not even close to the answer I want to hear.

"But the one thing that he did always talk about was his high school football team playing against Central High School on Thanksgiving Day at Hinchliffe Stadium [in Paterson], where the whole town stopped for that game. There were ten thousand people, standing room only. And I think they [Eastside High School] beat them all four years that he played. And those were some of his most cherished memories that he talked about all the time.

"But, you know, he was extremely proud of what he had done. And he knew that if Branch Rickey [the Brooklyn Dodgers executive who signed Jackie Robinson] and Mr. Robinson—which is how Dad would refer to him in public; he would say 'Jackie' to me—didn't do what they did, that Mr. [Bill] Veeck [who signed Doby to play for Cleveland] couldn't have done what he did. So, he was as happy as anyone else when the news came out that Jackie was going to sign, and he also knew that America did not change from April 15, 1947, to July 5, 1947."

One wonders why Doby Sr. was so reluctant to speak about the past.

"That's a question I can't answer. So, it's only speculation, you know? I would say that when he was in Paterson, he was in a little bit of a bubble. His teammates were his teammates. They walked to the movies together, they walked to school, they were in class. So [racism] wasn't in his face. After he left Paterson was when he had his first bouts with racism, segregation, integration, the Negro Leagues, the Navy, and Major League Baseball. As he got older, his lips got a little looser, and my nieces and great-nieces and nephews, they are privileged to have heard some of the stories, but I really didn't hear them."

Fortunately, Doby Sr.'s old teammates were more forthcoming.

"A lot of my information was from his teammates. I'll never forget, in 1977, my dad is coaching with the White Sox and Bob Lemon is the manager. And I couldn't wait to meet him, because there was a guy who played with my dad. And when I met him, I was probably nineteen years old and I said, 'Mr. Lemon, nice to meet you. Was my dad any good?' And he started laughing and I'm thinking, I wonder, what's so funny? And he goes, 'What do you mean?' I go, 'Well, was he good?' He goes, 'He was one of the best.' That's all I needed to hear."

During the 1978 season, Lemon was fired by team owner Bill Veeck and replaced by Larry Doby Sr. Doby himself was fired at the season's end.

"He wanted to [manage again]. He said he would have liked to have a full year, like a spring training and a full year to see how he could have done, but it didn't work out that way. But, you know what? He never questioned Mr. Veeck's decision because he said Mr. Veeck was like a father to him. He said he was a man of his word. You never had to decipher where he was coming from, or if he had an ulterior motive. So, he gave him a chance by hiring him. And then he didn't rehire him. He [my father] never questioned him. That's the love and respect he had for him. And, you know, there were some partial owners who probably didn't want my dad back, and that was it."

Given Veeck's relationship with Larry Sr., it must have been difficult for the owner to let Doby go after the 1978 season.

"It was, but it was just as difficult for him to fire Bob Lemon, you know? That's the business of baseball."

Did his dad ever offer advice about growing up Black in America?

"His thing was always to treat people as individuals and how they treat you. He felt that there were good people of all colors and faiths, and to judge them based on some broad kind of a lens was incorrect."

Around the house, Larry Doby Sr. was laid back, but also was "the enforcer."

"They [Mom and Dad] were always on a united front. My dad was the enforcer and Mom was his representative. We got spanked.

That was called discipline back in those days [laughs]. Mom was like, 'I'll tell your father.' You didn't want to hear those words. And, you know, even though I didn't see him play, he was away six months out of the year while I was growing up because he was coaching. And you sort of dread when he came back because you knew that 'the list' was going to be presented to him. But you were also happy because you were going to see him.

"But he was basically laid back. I remember, when certain things would make him laugh, we all thought it was great, 'cause he didn't laugh much, you know? His enjoyments were golf and his family and just coming home after six months on the road with baseball."

Larry Jr. tells a couple of stories that illustrate his dad's commitment to home and family.

"After he made the Hall of Fame, there was a pretty significant demand for his autograph. He had [an autograph show], let's say in Seattle, and he was booked for let's say three hours. Well, after three hours and he made like $5,000, there was still a line of people who wanted his autograph. And the promoter said, 'Hey, if you stay an extra two hours, we'll give you an extra $5,000.' And [Dad] says, 'No, that's okay, I'm good, thanks. I just want to get home. See my wife.' And I said to him, 'Excuse me, do you know how hard it is for me to make $5,000?' And he goes, 'I didn't care, Larry. I was ready to come home.' So, what ends up happening? The plane got delayed for two and a half hours. And he had to sit in the airport for free [laughs]."

Later, Larry Sr. was director of community relations for the New Jersey Nets basketball team (now the Brooklyn Nets).

"That was through Joe Taub, the owner. He grew up in Paterson with my father. He started ADP [Automatic Data Processing]. They were able to give back to Paterson through a thing called the Taub-Doby Basketball League, which went to the inner cities. They provided basketballs and shoes for the kids. When he retired from the Nets, they wanted to give him and my mother a trip to Europe. My mother was over the top. She couldn't wait to go. My father was like, 'I don't want to go to Europe.' And they didn't go. He was just a very basic guy who liked what he liked and, you know, that was the way he was."

Larry Jr. played baseball as a student at Duke University.

"[Dad] encouraged me, but it was always about the books. Not getting an education was not an option. So, yes, he was supportive but not over-supportive or over-coaching. He left so much to my coaches. I think he realized how difficult it is to make it in baseball and he knew that an education can never be taken away from you. That was one. And, two, there were some ballplayers who sort of pushed their kids and maybe the kids resented the game and their fathers. And he was 180 degrees the other way. He was like, 'I'm not going to do that to my son.'"

Larry Jr. was a switch-hitting outfielder.

"I started out as a first baseman in Little League and made some errors on ground balls and got moved to the outfield. I [became a switch-hitter] on my own. And I remember [Dad] was like, 'Oh, that's pretty good. It looks good.' You know, you feel proud."

At Duke, Doby's coach was Enos Slaughter, the former major league outfielder who reportedly was among the more vocal players opposed to Jackie Robinson joining the Dodgers.

"When I told my father that Duke was looking at me, he was over the moon. I got contacted first through football and didn't even know who the baseball coach was because football was going to be paying for my scholarship. But at some point in the recruiting process, they said we think we're going to make your scholarship half and half; you can get the rest of your money through baseball. And that's when I found out who the coach was. And I told my dad. He kind of looked at me a little weird, but then he had to put up or shut up with his statement of 'treat people the way they treat you, not the way they treated me' or whatever."

And how did it go with Coach Slaughter?

"It [the Robinson situation] wasn't discussed. I would have loved to have heard his take on it. I'll say this: All of us are products of our experiences and our environment. What he grew up with was segregation. Obviously, he carried that with him into baseball. But what I'll say is that my experiences with him were wonderful. He treated me well. I have nothing but good things to say about him. So, he either should be nominated for an Academy Award or, as I like to say, it doesn't matter where you start the race, it matters where you finish it. None of us are perfect. As you go through this journey called life and you meet people and listen and communicate and learn, [it's about] how do you process that information? And by the time I got to him in his life, he was a good dude."

Ironically, it turned out that Larry Jr. was the first Black baseball player at Duke.

"You know what? Those guys made me feel welcomed and never said, 'You're the first Black guy here.' I found that out years later."

Despite playing in the South, Larry Jr. says he didn't encounter anywhere near the level of racism that his father dealt with in his early days in the big leagues.

"I don't think I went through any more than any other player went through. Once, we played Valdosta State in Valdosta, Georgia, and in the outfield, there were all these pickup trucks lined with the stars and bars and the shotguns in the window. And [the people] sat on the hoods. I was playing the outfield and I'm looking around going, 'Where am I?' And I remember some guy saying, 'How are you doing today, boy?' And I said, 'I'm doing pretty good.' And that was it.

"Also, while we were there, there was an article in the paper of a fight between the Yankees and White Sox in 1957. Art Ditmar (a Yankee pitcher) threw a ball at my father's head. He charged the mound, and they started throwing punches. Enos was on the Yankees at that point. And, you know, everybody was going in defense of their teammates, and he jumped on my father and Walt Dropo (of the White Sox) pulled him off and ripped his shirt off. So, in the paper, while I was there, there was a big picture of Coach Slaughter in his Yankee uniform torn to shreds, walking away. And he never said a word to me about that. I thought that was kind of funny."

One thing Larry Jr. did hear were the comparisons with his dad.

"I heard all that stuff. Heard it everywhere. Every level I went, I heard it. I wouldn't say it didn't bother me at all, but it didn't bother me enough to deter me from what I was trying to do. One thing my parents said to me is that it's more important who you are than what you do."

After college, Larry Jr. played for Niagara Falls and Appleton in the White Sox organization from 1979 to 1981.

"I got drafted in my junior year. I wanted to [sign a pro contract]. I told my father I would go back to school [at a later date], and he said, 'You're not going to. You won't do it.' And, I mean, I obviously didn't make it, so maybe it was the right decision. The curveball got harder and harder to hit. And that was it."

Larry Jr. gave pro football a try.

"After a couple of years being out [of college], I signed with the USFL's [United States Football League, a professional league that played in the spring and summer from 1983 through 1985] Los Angeles Express. I signed, went out to L.A., and ended up tearing my hamstring and got let go. And then I was, like, alright, I guess it's time to start working."

Larry Jr. was a history major at Duke.

"I thought of possibly pursuing a career in law at some point. But when I graduated, I said I'm never going back to school."

And he didn't.

"So, I had this Duke degree and I'm getting all these interviews and everybody's wanting to talk to me, which was great, but all the interviews were like investment banking and Wall Street jobs. That's where my father was sort of hoping that I would end up. He had some friends in that business and they arranged some interviews.

And I was just like, I don't want to wear a tie every day to work. I went to Catholic school, and I wore a tie for four years and I was like, that doesn't seem like what I want to do. I thought if I started a job and I worked nine to five, forty hours a week, I would never pursue anything else. So, I said, I'm going to have to figure out something."

Enter Billy Joel, the musician.

"So, I started a job at the Meadowlands (in New Jersey) as a stage-hand. It wasn't every day, just a concert here, a concert there. I had a strong back and that's how I started out, unloading and loading trucks. Then, I learned more technical aspects of the job, such as rigging, sound, electrics, what have you. And I had a pretty good thing going on there for a while.

"And what happened was, Billy Joel and Bruce Springsteen used to come to the Meadowlands all the time. And their production manager who ran their road crews was a guy named Bob Thrasher. His nickname was Boomer. I ended up working with him a whole bunch of times. And one of my best friends at the Meadowlands was this guy, Vinnie, from Hackensack. So, Boomer asked Vinnie to go on a Springsteen tour and Vinnie liked it. And he said, 'Maybe you should try this.' And my first reaction was, 'Why do I want to do the same shit on the road that I'm doing at home when I can sleep in my own bed?' And he's like, 'It's fun. It's kind of cool, you should try it.'"

Eventually, he got an interview with Billy Joel.

"So, I came in and met him and we talked a little bit. Well, that job was to be Billy's valet. And Billy told them, 'I don't think I could ask that guy to fold my underwear.' So, I didn't get that job.

"But, eventually, a spot opened up [as a rigger on Joel's crew]. It didn't happen right away because Billy Joel treats his crew so good that people don't leave. So, that's how I started, and I've been with him twenty-five years or so.

"My father would always break my chops: 'You got a Duke education, and this is what you're doing?'"

In addition to his job on Billy Joel's crew, Larry Jr. works to preserve his dad's legacy. One such project was the initiative to restore Hinchliffe Stadium, the site of his dad's high school football exploits, former home to Negro League baseball, and now home to the New Jersey Jackals of the independent Frontier League.

"My father pretty much always had a soft spot for Paterson. So, when he was alive, he would do stuff for them. And, you know, when he passed on if they asked me to do something I would always try to make myself available.

"I think the toughest thing to do as the son of a public figure is to decide how to carry on the legacy when they're gone. I try my best to stay true to my father, who he was."

Larry Jr. spoke at Progressive Field in Cleveland when the Indians dedicated the statue of his father in 2015.

"I'll never forget this as long as I live. [My father] said he never got booed in Cleveland. And I looked at him like he was crazy. I'm

Larry Doby Jr. at the dedication of a statue in his dad's honor at Progressive Field in Cleveland. *AP Images*

like, 'They booed Mickey Mantle [in New York],' and he said, 'Nope, never got booed in Cleveland.' And I thought to myself, that speaks volumes of them. They felt like he was their guy. And then, also, they say integrity is what you do when nobody's looking. Cleveland was a little midwestern town and it wasn't a media focus or center like Brooklyn was for Jackie Robinson where they reported his every move. And they still treated my father that well. So, whenever they ask me to do something, I always go back and I always tell them that my father couldn't have done what he did without your support. And I thank them for it.

"The proudest thing I am of my dad is that he was one of the people who allowed little boys to dream. Before my father, a little kid of color didn't think, 'I want to grow up one day and be like so-and-so, to play in the big leagues.' It was the Negro League or nothing. So, because of what he did, a little kid could be sleeping in Birmingham, Alabama, and say, 'I want to be a big leaguer.'"

John Wathan and Dusty Wathan

Cup Ball and Stories from Buck O'Neil

Perhaps the number one backhanded compliment in baseball is this analysis of a catcher's footspeed: "He runs well . . . for a catcher."

John Wathan was an anomaly among catchers, though, because he ran well . . . period. In 1982, for example, Wathan stole 36 bases to break major league baseball's single-season record for a catcher, which had been 30, set by Ray Schalk in 1916. It should be noted that had Wathan not missed five weeks of the '82 season with a broken ankle, he almost certainly would have surpassed 40 steals (in case you're wondering, he didn't even come close to leading the league that season; Rickey Henderson swiped a record 130!). Proving 1982 was no fluke, Wathan stole 28 bags the following year, and 105 for his career.

Wathan was drafted in the first round by the Kansas City Royals out of the University of San Diego in 1971. He made his major league debut five years later and retired after the 1985 season. He was an anomaly in another sense, as he played his entire ten-year career for the Royals, an unusual achievement in the free agent era.

The 6-2, 205-pound right-handed batter played in two World Series for the Royals, losing to the Philadelphia Phillies in 1980 and defeating the St. Louis Cardinals in 1985, his final season. Wathan was an integral member of the 1980 American League champions, batting .305 in 510 plate appearances that year.

After his playing career, Wathan remained in the game as a major league coach with the Royals, California Angels, and Boston Red Sox. He managed the Royals from August 1987 until early in the 1991 campaign, and he was interim manager of the Angels for eighty-nine games in 1992.

He worked as an analyst on Royals television broadcasts in 1996 and 1997 and was a roving instructor for the team from 2006 to 2007. He was named a special assistant to the Royals' director of player development in 2008. He is, in short, a baseball lifer.

Nicknamed "Duke" for his entertaining impersonation of actor John Wayne, Wathan still lives in the Kansas City area with his wife, Nancy.

◆

It stands to reason that John Wathan, baseball lifer, would help raise a baseball family. John and Nancy Wathan had three children. The oldest, Dustin ("Dusty"), played for fourteen years in the minor leagues and had a brief major league cameo; Derek played eleven seasons in the minor leagues; and sister Dina Blevins is director of Community Investments/Alumni for the Kansas City Royals, for whom she has worked since 2005.

Dusty was born in August 1973 in Jacksonville, Florida, where his dad was playing for the Jacksonville Suns, a Royals minor league affiliate. Shortly after Dusty was born, his paternal grandfather—a pilot—picked up the family and flew them back to their winter home in Iowa.

"We lived in Iowa in the winter until I think I was in the third grade. My dad worked for his dad in the winter. Once I was old enough to go to school, my dad was in the big leagues. Then, I would start public school in Kansas City and then go to Catholic school in the winter in Iowa and finish [the school year] with the classes I started with back in public school in Kansas City.

"I don't remember [changing schools] being difficult at all. I think it was one of those things where, you know, young kids are adaptable. And then, after third grade, we moved to Kansas City full-time. He built a house in the middle of the [players'] strike in '81, so it was a little stressful for him. It was on about three-quarters of an acre, and there was supposed to be a cul-de-sac behind us. It was an old cornfield surrounded by some woods. And my dad bought the two lots behind him and our neighbor bought the two lots behind them. So, we put in like an eighty-yard football field and batting cages with a movable backstop because the guy next door was a big soccer player. So, we would set it up for soccer and baseball. It was the place to be, a great place in the wintertime, with four-wheelers being ridden and everything. And then in the summer, it was baseball and soccer, and in the fall, it was football.

"It was pretty neat. We had a place to play all the time. We didn't have to play in the street or anything like that. We were in a neighborhood with all the kids that I went to school with. So we always had a good group of people hanging out. My brother is three-and-a-half years younger than me. Between his age and my age, there was always a big group of kids playing something."

Despite having a baseball field in his own backyard, Dusty says there was no pressure from his dad to play the game.

"He always said, you guys do what you want to do. If you want to play piano, if you want to be a doctor, if you want to be a lawyer, just be happy and do what you enjoy. But, you know, going to the ballpark, being around the ballpark, watching so many games, you just develop a love for it. And you see that Dad loved the game and, you know, you want to do something that makes you happy and see it make your father and mother happy and pays the bills. Growing up, we played everything, but I really gravitated towards baseball when I got into high school."

Interestingly, Dusty didn't get a whole lot of baseball instruction from his dad.

"We really didn't do a lot of baseball stuff. More of it came from watching guys play and mimicking how [they] did things. When my dad was managing [the Royals], Glenn Ezell was the catching coach and bullpen coach, so Glenn and I would go out and do stuff. And Brent Mayne was the backup catcher at the time. And he'd go throw to me a couple of times a week. When Dad was home, it was football season, it was basketball season. It wasn't baseball season. My dad played college basketball, so the most coaching I ever got from him was in basketball."

Despite having a recognizable last name, Dusty says he didn't feel any particular pressure to live up to his dad's standard in baseball.

"The town we grew up in, Blue Springs, had a large population of players. Jamie Splittorff [son of Royals pitcher Paul] played on my baseball team, [also] Dennis Leonard Jr., Corey Otis, Cullen McRae [all sons of Royals players]. We all played together for a few years. Jamie and I were pretty much the only ones who stuck with baseball. Jamie ended up playing in college and a little bit in professional baseball in the minors.

"I was really lucky. I had some good coaches growing up that didn't really care who anybody's dad was. I had one coach all the way through, up until high school. We [the Philadelphia Phillies, for whom Dusty is a coach] did the Little League Classic [in 2018], and we got to write somebody's name on a patch on our sleeve. So, I wrote John Cain [Dusty's longtime youth coach] as the guy who was influential on me. I mean, my dad was, obviously, but you know how it is with travel and everything like that. You have to have somebody throw you in the back of a pickup truck back in the day and take you to practice. He was very influential and supportive of everything that we did."

One year, Dusty and his teammates played in the American Amateur Baseball Congress championship game, losing to South Gate, California.

"I think we were twelve years old. It was funny because it was in Rockford, Illinois. The Royals were in Chicago that week. And the next thing you know, you looked up in the stands and there was Amos [Otis], and Paul Splittorff, Dennis Leonard, and my dad. They all got a chance to come down and watch us play that day. That was pretty cool. Back in those days, they didn't get Saturday [afternoons] off very often. They were pretty good at the time, so I remember a lot of years when I was growing up, they were the Saturday *Game of the Week*."

For younger fans of today's game, who can watch any team at any time, it might be difficult to comprehend that for many years the Saturday *Game of the Week*, on NBC, was the one opportunity for fans to see games not involving their hometown teams, other than the postseason. It also gave Dusty a lifetime memory.

"I think I was like seven or eight years old. I used to go on the road with my dad once a year. Jamie Splittorff and I would usually go together. We'd be batboys or whatever. [One day], we got to announce the *Game of the Week* starting lineup, in Baltimore. It was pretty cool."

At school, Dusty seldom, if ever, heard remarks about his dad's performance the night before.

"I grew up in a small town and the Royals were good, so maybe that helped. It was the Midwest, not New York City. I can imagine that growing up in New York or somewhere like that would have been a different story, but I don't ever remember running into a problem with kids. I was just one of the guys. My buddy's dad was an attorney, and my dad was a baseball player, and it was just kind of how we did things. That was my normal. [People] ask, 'What was it like growing up with a baseball player as a father?' And you're like,

'Well, I don't know, what's it like growing up with a plumber as a father?' It's the only thing I know. I can't compare it to anything."

At home, Dusty says the Royals "were big on family."

"We were lucky. A lot of days, we would go to the ballpark with our dad early. Back then, you just kind of had the run of the ballpark. The security situation wasn't much. I knew everybody around the stadium, ushers and ticket people and security. We'd run around the stadium, shag BP [batting practice], hit in the cages, just everything. It was a good time.

"I was in the clubhouse all the time. It was a lot less corporate [than today]. There were people coming in and out and it really taught you where your place was. Like, we knew when to stay and hang out, and when to disappear.

Dusty Wathan joins his dad on the field in Kansas City. *Dusty Wathan*

"We used to play cup ball all the time in the bottom of Royals Stadium [hitting a wadded-up paper cup that served as a ball]. We used to just play for hours and hours down there. And, you know, it was no big deal. Like, my mom didn't worry. She knew that when the game was over, we'd show up. I got to watch the games from behind home plate with scouts, so I learned a lot that way, just talking to guys. I probably drove those guys crazy. Buck O'Neil [former player and manager in the Negro Leagues and a Hall of Famer], I used to sit with all the time. The stories I heard from [him] were just amazing. He was an unbelievable storyteller. I look back on it and I'm like, 'Wow, I was getting a serious education on the history of baseball.' It doesn't get much better than that at about eight, nine, ten years old."

One special time in the clubhouse occurred when the Royals won the World Series in 1985.

"This is kind of a testament to my mom. Dean Vogelaar was the Royals PR guy at the time. And we were outside the locker room. I was thirteen or so. And Dean says, 'Alright, the wives can come in the clubhouse now.' And my mom says, 'No, no, my boys are going in. I don't need to go in there.' So, we got to go into the clubhouse first. I'm sure my mom came in later, but I just remember the players were happy to see us because, you know, we were in the clubhouse every day and we were kind of part of it, in a sense. It was neat to be able to go in there and get dumped in a cart and for beer to be poured on you at thirteen years old."

On the road trips, his dad tried to instill life lessons in his son.

"I remember being in New York and getting into the cab to go to Yankee Stadium, and my dad told the cabbie, 'Take us through Harlem.' And the cabbie said, 'I don't really want to do that.' [Dad] said, 'I'll pay you extra. Just take us through Harlem. I want to show him [Dusty] what it's like.' I learned a lot from different places. We went to Baltimore; we'd go to the Inner Harbor. We went to Boston; we'd do Paul Revere's ride. So, he took me on all those neat vacation things that a lot of people don't do. It really taught me a lot through my minor league career and where I'm at now to just take advantage of where you are at the time. That was one thing he taught me, 'Hey, let's experience some things.'"

Dusty says those formative years led to some lifelong friendships.

"My dad and George Brett [former Royals third baseman and a Hall of Famer] were roommates in the minor leagues and in spring training for years. George used to come over for Thanksgiving. Jamie Quirk [former Royals player] is my brother's godfather. Kevin Seitzer is a hitting coach for the Braves. I've known 'Seitz' since I was a little kid.

"When we were growing up, you'd wake up the next morning and there'd be guys laying on the couch because back then there was no food really in the locker room right after the game. You were on your own. My mom was always making sandwiches after the game. We always had our big meal at like noon or one o'clock all summer. That was our dinner. We'd eat that before my dad went to the ballpark and then after the game, we would have sandwiches or whatever. I can remember guys coming over after the game for a barbecue and hanging out, and just ended up staying the night. A lot of those guys weren't married and didn't have kids yet, and my mom was the one kind of taking care of everybody."

Later, when his dad was managing the Royals, he had to play the role of enforcer.

"He had a kind of get-together for the players [at our house]. I was in high school then. Most of the team was there. The next thing you know, a basketball game broke out with Bret Saberhagen [a Royals pitcher] and a bunch of guys. It probably freaked my dad out a little bit. And he's like, 'Okay, that's it, no more basketball.' He had two-thirds of his starting rotation out there playing and [could] see somebody getting hurt. So, here comes this grumpy old guy telling us we can't play basketball. And now it's a little circle, 'cause I see that with my players back when I was managing in the minor leagues, I'd freak out too [laughs].

"It's kind of crazy now that it's starting to come full circle for me. One example is I saw Daulton Varsho [a player on the Arizona Diamondbacks] this summer. Well, Gary [Daulton's father] was a coach with the Phillies when I first came over here as a player. And so, I knew Daulton when he was a tiny kid, probably like four years old. And I go up to him and I said, 'Hey, I know this is crazy, but I met you when you were four years old. This is what my life has been like, so this is probably what your life is going to be like.'"

His dad's playing career ended with the 1985 World Series.

"He went to spring training in '86 and I guess he was the last guy let go. They asked him to stay on, so what he did was he sat in the stands for the first three games of the season and cleared waivers. And then they asked him to stay on the major league staff. He was kind of the assistant bullpen coach at the time, and then [manager] Dick Howser was diagnosed with a brain tumor and had to step down. Everybody got shifted around. My dad went to coach first base for the rest of the season, and then they asked him to go manage in the minor leagues in '87. In August of '87, they hired him [to manage the major league club]."

"We'd eat before he went to the ballpark, and I would grill him with questions. He said I was worse than the media sometimes. I would ask him, like, 'Last night, why did you hit and run there? Why didn't you run there? What happened there? Why did you take him out of the game?' There were a lot of conversations like that, especially through high school."

Dusty often accompanied his dad on promotional appearances away from the ballpark.

"He had a couple of car deals. That was real commonplace back then. You'd go sign autographs for an hour and they gave you a car for a month or two. We did a lot of charity stuff. My dad hosted a cerebral palsy telethon for years and years in Kansas City; Nick Lowry [former Kansas City Chiefs placekicker] and him. We also did bowl-a-thons. Dad was really good about showing us what everybody's life is like, about how good we have it, and that we're so fortunate. Like the story about Harlem. I look back on it and see how special that was and how cool it was that my dad said, 'This is where we are. Let's show you guys what it's like to grow up in another walk of life, whether that's a disability or poverty or whatever it may be, so you guys can help people one day.'"

Winter in the Wathan house was a special time.

"[Dad] would wake us up for breakfast every day. He'd be there when we got home from school. So, that was great. He coached our basketball teams, and we went to a lot of Chiefs games. It was a lot of family time together. We tried to get out to San Diego once or twice in the wintertime. Both my parents grew up in San Diego, so my grandma was out there. We didn't travel a ton, I think because my dad traveled so much during the season that he wanted to enjoy home and, with kids, we had school and were busy doing our sports stuff."

San Diego was the site of a family tragedy in June 1979 when John Wathan's mother was murdered by his thirty-four-year-old step-brother, who suffered from mental health issues.

"Dad did a really good job of hiding that from us kids. He didn't really talk about it and just said that she had passed away and, you know, being five or six years old, you just didn't really ask questions. At five or six years old, you don't need to know that. Later, I was in middle school or high school, my dad kind of sat us down and told us the story of what happened.

"Things happen to families everywhere. Nobody has a perfect life. You pull back the curtain, things happen to everybody no matter what it looks like from the outside."

On the ballfield, Dusty, like his dad, became a catcher.

"I played shortstop, third base, pitcher, right field, catcher. But eventually, you get to a spot where [they say], 'We gotta put you somewhere. You can't run [laughs], so you'll catch.'"

In 1994, Dusty signed as an amateur free agent with the Seattle Mariners out of Cerritos College. That began a baseball odyssey that took him through seven organizations over a fourteen-year period.

"My goal was to sign a pro contract and play long enough to have a little bit of credibility to coach. I didn't think I was good enough to play at a high level for a long period of time. I had a couple of decent years that helped me along the way, but I think being a good teammate and being healthy for most of my career helped me to play for fourteen years."

Dusty's perseverance paid off in 2002 when he got called to the major leagues by the Royals that September. He doubled in his first major league at-bat and went three for five over three games, good for a .600 batting average. "I am one of the few guys who would like to lower his career batting average [laughs]."

His dad witnessed Dusty's major league debut in person.

"It was in Kansas City. He was sitting behind the plate. But it was bittersweet. It was a weird season. I started with San Diego and got traded to Milwaukee at the end of spring training, and I went to AA with Milwaukee and got hurt. They put me on the seven-day DL [disabled list]. When seven days passed, they wouldn't activate me. I went in and said, 'Hey, I'm twenty-eight years old,' or whatever the heck I was at the time, 'and I need to play, I can't sit here any longer.'"

The Milwaukee organization granted Dusty his release and he signed with Kansas City, which assigned him to their triple-A club in Omaha.

"The [minor league] season ends, and Kansas City doesn't call up a third catcher. They're like the only team in baseball that didn't call up a third catcher in September. My wife's Canadian. So, we flew up there to see her parents. I was on a golf course in Canada with no cell service at the time. I just teed off and this guy comes out and I'm thinking, 'Geez, what did we do?' And he says, 'You need to make a phone call home to your mother and father's house.' So, I called them. They said Muzzy Jackson from the Royals called. They needed me to go to Detroit because [Royals catchers] A. J. Hinch's and Brent Mayne's wives were both due the same day. I went to Detroit, and they didn't activate me for that series. We went back to Kansas City, and I got activated. But at that time, my wife was due. We already had one daughter, and my son was due in November. She was in Arizona, where we lived at the time. So, she was on the bed listening to it through the internet while she was eight months pregnant. So, that was kind of bittersweet. But it was neat being in Kansas City. I had some friends there. My parents were there, my brother, his sister . . . everybody was there. Not many guys hit a double in their first game ever and go back to their parents' house and sit with their dad and have a beer in the house they grew up in."

By the next season, though, Dusty was back in the minor leagues.

"My last year was '07. I was thirty-four years old. John Russell was my manager. Around July, I said, 'I think I'm done. I think this is it.' He knew I wanted to coach, and he basically showed me the ropes. He sat me down at the computer; this is how you write reports, this is what we're looking for. We were in Richmond one day and he took me out to third base. 'This is how you coach third base. You stand here in this situation'; started going over situations. It just worked out—I got a job with Philly the next year.

"I managed all the way through the system. And for the last three or four years, like 2015, '16, '17 or so, I would finish the season in the big leagues. They would send me up in September to be an extra coach. Well, they told Pete Mackanin [Phillies manager] that he wasn't coming back for the '18 season. I interviewed for the manager's job, and it came down to Gabe Kapler and myself, and Kap won the job. So, that was a disappointment, obviously. But then, right away, Kap said, 'I want you to be on the staff.' So, that was kind of bittersweet. I lost out on the manager's job but got my chance to coach in the big leagues."

Dusty says he still harbors aspirations to follow in his dad's footsteps by managing in the major leagues.

"That's what I want to do one day. I interviewed for the Texas job when [Chris] Woodward got [it]. That was in '19. Hopefully, I'll get a couple more shots and get the job one day. It's like being in the right place at the right time. A lot of times you see guys that were really, really good players never make it to the big leagues. And you see guys that you thought were just kind of alright, and they make it to the big leagues for a while. You just have to be in the right place at the right time. I always tell players that everybody has a window, it's just that some windows are bigger than others. You just gotta be able to take advantage of that window when it opens."

Dusty and his wife, Heidi, live in Matthews, North Carolina, a suburb of Charlotte. They have two girls and two boys. Their oldest son, Huck, plays baseball at the University of Charlotte.

As his father raised him, Dusty says he never pushed his sons into baseball.

"People would be surprised at how little we talk baseball. After his games, my first question is, 'Did you have fun?' Yeah, okay. 'Did you win?' Okay. 'How'd you do?' That's how it goes. My biggest thing is that they're having fun. I don't care about anything else, to be honest."

Henry Rodriguez and David Rodriguez

Seeking Dad's Acceptance: "All I Wanted Was a Barbie"

Baseball aficionados know all about the Reggie Bars that were thrown on the Yankee Stadium field by fans on April 13, 1978, when Reggie Jackson homered in the Bronx Bombers' home opener.

But even the most ardent baseball fans probably don't know—or have long forgotten—that another, albeit less famous, slugger was showered with post-home run candy bars on a regular basis.

That confection-feted player was Henry Rodriguez, a 6-1, 180-pound outfielder/first baseman who played eleven seasons in the big leagues with the Los Angeles Dodgers (1992–1995), Montreal Expos (1995–1997 and 2002), Chicago Cubs (1998–2000), Florida Marlins (2000), and New York Yankees (2001). For his career, the left-handed hitting Rodriguez hit 160 home runs with an on-base + slugging (OPS) percentage of .802.

It was during his first stint with Montreal that Rodriguez began to shine. In 1996, he set what was then an Expos team record with thirty-six home runs to go along with an .887 OPS, earning him a place on that summer's National League all-star team, his first and only all-star selection.

Fans began handing Oh Henry! bars to Rodriguez after games, but by late spring a new ritual had begun: They started tossing them on the field after a Rodriguez home run or other big hit. The practice continued into the next season and even followed him for a time while he was playing for the Cubs starting in 1998.

And it proved lucrative for the Dominican-born Rodriguez, who for a time served as a paid spokesperson for the Hershey Company treat.

Rodriguez followed up his first big year with the Expos with 26 home runs for the team in 1997, 31 and 26 for the Cubs in 1998 and 1999, respectively, and 20 for the Cubs and Marlins in 2000, averaging just under 28 per season during the five-year span. That improbable power surge accounted for 139 of his 160 career home runs.

From there, the fall was swift. He had only eight plate appearances in a brief stint with the Yankees early in the 2001 season, and twenty-five plate appearances in an early-season reunion with the Expos in 2002. On May 16, 2002, Rodriguez was released by the Expos at the age of thirty-four. He went on to play in the Mexican and independent leagues from 2004 to 2006, but he never did make it back to the major leagues.

◆

David Rodriguez's relationship with his father can best be described as cordial. That is not to say there isn't love there, but the father-son connection is missing one very critical bond: Dad's acknowledgment of his son's identity as a gay man. The two have never had a meaningful conversation about it.

Born in April 1995, David was just a toddler when Oh Henry! bars rained down from the stands in Montreal and Chicago. His memories of his dad's baseball career are confined mostly to Henry's stints playing winter ball for Tigres del Licey in the Dominican Republic.

"I remember going on weekends. My mom would take me to the games. [Dad] would take me into the locker room and all that stuff. He always wanted me to be a baseball player, or just something with baseball because he loved it so much. And I don't blame him. He would take me to the batting cages; that would be his quality time with me. The thing that he knew how to do was anything related to baseball. So, it was pretty interesting because I'm not a baseball person. It's never been something that interested me."

David didn't get to see his dad much as a young boy growing up in the Dominican Republic.

"We didn't spend too much time together. He was always busy, and when I got to see him, it would be like for a little bit. I remember, for Christmas, he would bring a bunch of toys and all that. He was a caring father. It's just that, you know, sometimes people don't necessarily know how to show that much affection. And then your child is different. I'm gay. So, for him, that came as like, not necessarily a shock because I feel that he always knew, but I feel that parents either acknowledge it or choose not to; just ignore it and be like, okay, maybe it's a phase or something.

"It was always like a block for him to try to bond with me because, with his oldest son (David's step-brother), he was into sports; a guy's guy, you know what I mean? He was into baseball. So, [Dad] had a really strong connection with a son. So, when I came around, it was like, 'I don't know how to handle this.' It was always interesting to me, whenever he would come, he would always bring gifts, and the gifts would be baseball-related. It would be very superficial in a way. He didn't necessarily know how to approach me in a way he knew how to approach his other son. I was like, okay, the baseball is cute, but honestly, I'd rather play with Barbie."

Apart from the time demands of a baseball career, David says his dad was occupied with another relationship.

"[My parents] weren't legally separated, but I knew he had another relationship. That was something that I knew of, but we never really talked about it. He was always working, or when he wasn't working, he was probably with the other lady. [My parents] didn't get legally divorced until I was about twelve, thirteen years old. That's when [Mom and I] moved to New York.

"He was never really a full-time dad. It's not like he was never there because he would always stop by even for a little bit. But it was a bit awkward because you don't know what to do. You don't want it to be awkward. You're my dad and we're supposed to be close. But it was never a bad time because he was always a very sweet guy."

David's mom, Patricia, told Henry that his son is gay.

"My mom said that she knew when I was like three. She would tell [Dad]. It wasn't until my great-grandmother from my mom's side passed away and he came for a visit (to New York) that I actually remember them having that conversation. I heard them.

"He was like, 'What's going on with him?' And [Mom] was like, 'Your son is gay.' Even though he knew, it still came as a shock to him when [she] said it to him again. You could see it in his face. But he was never mean about it. I'm very lucky in the sense that it was never anything dramatic."

David and his mom had a long conversation about it when he was around sixteen years old.

"We went to TGI Fridays [laughs]. She asked me, 'Are you dating anybody?' And I was like, 'No.' She was like, 'Any boyfriends?' I was like, 'No,' and she was like, 'Would you like to have a boyfriend?' And I was like, 'Sure, one day, why not?' So, it was the most casual conversation. It wasn't like a Lifetime original movie or anything; we were just eating. She was asking questions because I never verbalized it to her. But, I mean, when you're ten years old and your favorite artist is Barbra Streisand, there's a question that needs to be asked [laughs]."

On the contrary, David's sexuality remains a mostly unspoken subject between father and son.

"I did have a quick conversation with him about it, but there's just something about it when you know somebody's not going to be able to fully understand it. They can tolerate it. They can hang out with you and all that stuff. But there are just some people that will never understand, and it'll always seem alien to them or something.

So, I just know that he's that type of guy. Not to say that he's a mean person or anything, because he's not. He always did the best he could with what he knew.

"Hopefully, I'll get to talk to him about it at some point. Even though we don't have the strongest, the closest, relationship. I do talk to him every once in a while. He'll call me just to see how I'm doing. I feel like it would be almost cathartic for me to have that conversation with him, just to see his perspective on things. I know how I felt, but I could only imagine how he felt as a dad. So, even though he does know, for me, it's just a matter of he was never comfortable talking about that with me; he didn't know what to say. He didn't know how to approach it. Hopefully, one day, we'll be able to have that conversation. I just hope he's able to at least understand a bit."

Still, David recalls his childhood in a positive way.

"I grew up very fortunate. I went to the best schools in the Dominican Republic. I lived in a beautiful home. He provided more than enough in terms of money. He was always there in that sense, for school and all of that."

Things did get rocky for a while, though, when his parents divorced.

"It got very ugly, in a way, in terms of money. That's always something that will bring out the ugly in people. My mom had always been a housewife. When she met my dad, he wanted her to be at home and take care of the home and take care of me. So, for her, it was always being with me. She'd take me to school, take me to every extracurricular thing that she could think of—karate, painting, swimming, dancing—she would always keep me busy. She had actually gone to school to be a teacher, so when she knew the divorce was coming, she got a job as a teacher at a Montessori School in the Dominican Republic. She knew that if she wasn't going to be able to support me based on my dad's money, that she was going to have to get a job and support me."

Today, Henry Rodriguez has homes in the Dominican Republic and Pennsylvania, according to his son. David, meanwhile, has carved out a niche for himself in the world of YouTube, where he posts humorous commentaries about movies under the name ZZA-VID. He has more than 150,000 subscribers.

"I haven't seen him in a long time because he doesn't really come to New York that much. We'll talk every once in a while. [We'll] have pretty quick conversations, nothing too personal because he's not very talkative at all; you know, very old-school kind of dad kind of vibe. So, I know my bounds with him in a way."

David's mom remarried several years after her divorce from Henry.

"[My step-dad] knows everything about me and he's very comfortable talking about it. I actually feel like I have more of a father-son relationship with him than I do with my actual dad. It's pretty nice. It's like a new chapter in her life and, you know, in a way, I got another father."

But still, that unspoken void, the "pink elephant in the room" as David calls it, lingers in David's memory.

"The most important thing I wish I had from a father wasn't necessarily he always had to be there for all of the school events or anything, but I feel that it would have been nice to have a father that was at least understanding enough to know that, yeah, your son is different. I always remember—and this is gonna sound so silly—but as a kid, I always wanted a Barbie. That sounds so silly, and so ridiculous, I know, but I always wanted a Barbie, and I would get everything on [my] list except for the Barbie. And I asked my mom, when I got older, why I never got the Barbie. And it was because, 'Your father never wanted to get you the Barbie.' And it bothered me for the longest time. I always wondered, why would a toy bother him so much?

"I was just so confused. That was the only thing that I actually went to therapy for. Growing up, I never understood why a father

David and Henry Rodriguez during Henry's days in Montreal. *David Rodriguez*

would deny his child something that brings him joy or pleasure. It's a child's toy. But, for some reason, it's those little things that stick with you. It's a toy, who cares? But as a kid, it was something that I remember. Saying it out loud sounds ridiculous, but it's just something that I never understood.

"I feel like, growing up, when I was able to put words into what I feel, it was like the acceptance. Like I feel that he could not accept me. And I always felt like that was the wall. I feel like, if he was able to say, 'Sure, get the Barbie,' I feel that would have put us in a much healthier position. Now, I'm able to intellectualize it, but for the longest time I just never understood [it].

"I feel that we missed a good opportunity because he's such a nice guy. I feel that if he was just able to feel uncomfortable for a little bit, we would've had a good breakthrough in our relationship. Sometimes I hear it in his voice, where he feels kind of bad. Like there's a little bit of guilt in there somewhere.

"I have a picture of my dad taking me onto the field. He would always tell me this story because I always saw it in pictures, but he told me my mom was there, and he took me to the field and the crowd was just going crazy and all the baseball players would bring their sons and daughters to the field. Every time he [told] that story, he would just get so excited. And so emotional, almost, which is like the rare time that I would see him emotional. He would tell me how he took me to the middle of the field and everybody cheering and roaring. He always said he felt like a rock star at that moment."

Despite not being a baseball fan, David acknowledges having some sentimental attachment to the sport.

"I do enjoy going to baseball games just because I feel like it's almost a childhood thing that you kind of connect with. I do like going whenever I can. Not that I necessarily knew everything that was going on, but it was simply because it was just very comforting. I always admired how hard [Dad] had to work. He was just so dedicated to baseball. And I feel that it gave me an appreciation for him that otherwise I probably wouldn't have had."

Mariano Rivera and Jafet Rivera

"Come on, Rivera, Throw the Cutter"

Who was the greatest hitter of all time: Babe Ruth? Ty Cobb? Ted Williams? Tony Gwynn?

Who was the greatest starting pitcher of all time: Walter Johnson? Sandy Koufax? Bob Gibson? Greg Maddux?

Who was the greatest closer of all time? Mariano Rivera . . . period.

When it comes to discussions of the greatest of all time in baseball, or any sport, there is room for considerable debate and, indeed, countless hours have been spent doing just that in taverns and living rooms across the country.

But when it comes to closers, the discussion usually starts and ends with one man: Mariano Rivera.

Rivera made his mark as the closer for the New York Yankees from 1997 through 2013, a period in which the team won four World Series and made the postseason "tournament" in all but two seasons. He was named World Series Most Valuable Player in 1999 and American League Championship Series MVP in 2003.

To be fair, in any given regular season during Rivera's remarkable run with the Yankees there were others around baseball who were just as good, and in some cases even better. But Rivera stood alone in his longevity and postseason greatness. His ability to remain at the top of his craft for such a prolonged period of time and to take his game to an other-worldly level in the playoffs is what set him apart from the rest.

In the postseason, Rivera pitched to an astounding 0.70 earned run average across ninety-six games and 141 innings, with forty-two saves (a record, and an apropos one at that, since 42 was Rivera's uniform number). Postseason opposing lineups, by definition, are generally among the best and deepest in the game, and of course, the late innings of these games are pressure-cookers. Yet Rivera somehow elevated his performance. His regular-season career ERA was 2.21, the lowest in the live-ball era among qualified pitchers, but that's still three times higher than his postseason mark.

The Panama native was a thirteen-time all-star and five-time World Series champion (four as the team's closer and one, in 1996, as the set-up man for closer John Wetteland). Rivera holds the major league record for most career saves, 652, and finished in the top three in the Cy Young Award voting four times. And it was all done with essentially one pitch, his signature cut fastball.

His accomplishments and standing among his peers were recognized when he was voted into the Hall of Fame's class of 2019 in his first year of eligibility as the first—and still the only—unanimous selection by the Baseball Writers' Association of America. His induction ceremony was attended by an estimated fifty-five thousand people, including Laurentino Cortizo, the president of Panama, where Rivera can best be described as a living legend.

A devout Christian, "The Sandman" was presented with the Presidential Medal of Freedom in 2019 in recognition of his charitable work, which includes the Mariano Rivera Foundation.

◆

Jafet Rivera is the second of three sons born to Mariano and Clara Rivera, entering the world in 1997, the year his father started his long run as the closer for the Yankees. Jafet was born in Panama but moved with his family to Westchester County in New York when he was three or four years old. It didn't take long for him to figure out that his father wasn't a regular suburban dad.

"Early on, I knew he was very different from all the fathers because he wasn't able to be there for the little things, like if there was a father-son thing at school, or a play, or a graduation from elementary school and things like that, or like, parents would just come and pick up their kid from school and things like that. I knew that he was different because he couldn't go to those things. And then all the teachers, they would be like, 'Oh, how's your dad? Tell your dad I said good game.' Or, 'Your dad did great last night.' I think it was second grade when I knew, okay, Dad's an athlete and he has to do this. I just understood that it was just part of my life, you know? I wasn't going to grow up the way that all the other kids grew up.

"We couldn't really go anywhere and have privacy. Everybody always recognized him and asked for a picture or an autograph. Sometimes I [liked it] because it was like, oh, cool, they're asking my dad for a picture, an autograph. But most of the time, it was like, man, I just don't want to share [him] right now. I don't want anybody to come, I just want him for myself. I just want this time to get to really talk to him about how he's doing and for me to express how I'm doing. And so, we really didn't get that part, you know? My close friends knew that my life was different. One time, a friend went out [with our family] for dinner. He got to experience my life, and he was like, 'You do this? This is crazy!'

"Of course, there were so many great things that I've been privileged and blessed to be a part of. For starters, you have the greatest of all time as your dad. That's just to start. And then, the house, the places you get to eat at, the places you get to go to, the people you get to meet. It was just surreal. But then, it's also difficult sometimes, where it was like, okay, I just want to hang out with Dad and I just want to chill, you know? But I couldn't 'cause he had to go. He would leave in the morning, maybe like nine, and then would come home at around 11 [at night].

"So, when we were growing up, we really didn't get to see him that much. It would be like periods, days, where we would spend like very few times with him unless you went to the stadium. That was when we got to see him for a little bit. And, for me, I'll always cherish those moments. I think the most memories that I have growing up are the old stadium [the Yankees moved out of their original stadium after the 2008 season], predominantly because of the relationships that I've formed with other players' kids. I spent more than half my life at Yankee Stadium. I was super close with Bernie [Williams's] kids, Andy Pettitte's kids. We would go to this playroom [at the ballpark] and my brother and I would stay there until like the seventh inning. And then my mom would come in and she would grab us and would take us up in the stands to see him [pitch]. The thing is, we wouldn't want to go because we were young; we just wanted to play. We played wall ball in there. But when they won, we got to go see him in the clubhouse. So, when the Yankees won, the song would come on [Frank Sinatra's "New York, New York"] and we would run down [to the clubhouse].

"There was this entrance that we would go down. You could smell like the paint, like the stairs had a certain type of smell to it. And the clubhouse was just awesome because when you got in, you see all the players lined up and they're high-fiving. So, me and my brother, we would sneak in and just high-five the players. So, that was definitely fun. I mean, you saw guys like [Derek] Jeter, Hideki [Matsui], A-Rod [Alex Rodriguez], [Jason] Giambi, Jorge [Posada], Alfonso Soriano, all these great guys. Paul O'Neill, Tino [Martinez], like everybody's there."

The players' kids weren't allowed in the clubhouse after a loss, but "they won a lot, so there weren't many days that we didn't get to go in."

Sometimes, Dad's baseball pals would come by the Rivera house in Westchester.

"He was very good friends with Ramiro Mendoza [a pitcher]. He'd come over the house. Bernie Williams and Jorge [Posada] would come over, too. It was routine. To me, it was just like my parents' friends, you know? When I'd go on road trips, that's when it would hit me. It was like, I'm really with these guys! When we got old enough to where we could actually go on the plane with the team, he took us to like four or five away trips. My favorite was when we went to the West Coast when they played Seattle, San Francisco, and L.A. I loved those. You're on the plane with the whole team. The manager was in front with the coaches. My dad would always be in the middle and then the back was always nuts."

Jafet played some baseball himself, an experience that he says was "crazy."

"In Little League, I had no care in the world. It's Little League, everybody's just hitting the ball, running around the bases. I was always an athlete. I was always fast, and I knew how to play ball. Travel ball, I guess when I got to middle school, you started to have tryouts and things like that, and that's when it started to become, instead of fun, more of an expectation. That's when it started. People would come to the games, and they would already know who I was. I was a pitcher, so there's already an expectation of being the next big thing. And it's like, I just wanted to have fun, you know? I just wanted to play the game. And so, as the years progressed, I just started noticing that I put more and more pressure on myself because of the pressure that people put on me. Like, there were literally games when parents would be chanting, 'Come on Rivera, throw the cutter.' And it's like, are you serious? I'm thirteen. Thirteen! What do you want from me? I just threw fastballs. That's all my dad ever taught me, just throw a fastball.

"Dad wouldn't give me a tremendous amount of advice. I don't think he really wanted to push or force anything on me. I think in some sort of way he knew that we already had a lot of pressure on our backs. It was so stressful when he would come to a game. So stressful. The last game that I ever played baseball was in my junior year of high school. And I did terrible. And I just never played again. I mean, I knew I could pitch, but after that game, I was just so tired [of baseball]. Plus, I wanted to do soccer more. But it was just a brutal game, and it was just embarrassing. And this is high school, so kids don't care what they say. So, they're chirping and it was crazy. It was definitely crazy. I mean, [Dad's] not just a regular ballplayer. He was a mega-celebrity. I didn't want to have to pretend to live up to something that I wasn't. I wasn't going to do that."

Jafet Rivera (right) with his dad Mariano and Mariano Jr. at the All-Star Game. *Jafet Rivera*

Today, Jafet is working on completing his college degree and helps run events for the Mariano Rivera Foundation. Most of his extended family still lives in Panama. Pre-COVID, Jafet and his immediate family would try to visit Panama at least once a year, which he describes as an experience unlike any other.

"When we go back there, it's a whole other level. My older brother, he went to school in Panama before we moved to the states, and there were threats to kidnap him. And so, my dad had to get a security guard. That's how it was. When you talk about Dad being famous here in the states, it's a whole other thing over there in Panama. Like, literally, the whole country idolizes him. We can't go anywhere."

Is there any place the Riveras can go and not be stopped by fans?

"We went to Europe and not that many people recognized him. So, it was cool. It was fun. People there don't really recognize him and don't watch so much baseball; it was the best. But it doesn't matter where we are in the world, *someone's* going to stop him."

Despite the unique challenges, Jafet says he wouldn't change anything about his childhood.

"I wouldn't change anything because the lifestyle that we had and the way that we grew up made me into the person that I am today. I think I've learned a lot of lessons from just watching [Dad] and just from being around him, even at the ballpark, like things about the game that I could put into something else in everyday life. There was a lot of good, and there was bad, but you learn from those. I learned to appreciate those moments because they were moments of growth."

Vada Pinson and Vada Pinson III

Yearning for a Father's Love

Unless you are a real student of baseball history, Vada Pinson probably falls into the category of "one of the greatest players you've never heard of."

How good was Vada Pinson?

The left-handed hitter compiled 2,757 career hits, essentially less than a season-and-a-half's worth of production from the 3,000 mark that generally punches a player's ticket into the Hall of Fame in Cooperstown. He hit 256 career home runs, had four 200-hit seasons (two of which led the National League), stole 305 bases, and won a Gold Glove Award for his defense in centerfield. Emblematic of his dynamic combination of power and speed were the five seasons in which he hit 20 or more home runs and stole 20 or more bases.

Pinson played in the major leagues from 1958 to 1975. His prime years came with his first team, the Cincinnati Reds, which inducted him into their Hall of Fame in 1977. In his final seasons, he played for the St. Louis Cardinals, Cleveland Indians, California Angels, and Kansas City Royals.

Following his playing career, from 1977 to 1994, Pinson served on the coaching staffs of the Seattle Mariners, Chicago White Sox, Detroit Tigers, and Florida Marlins.

Pinson's abilities extended beyond baseball: He was a talented musician who considered playing the trumpet for a living before the Reds came calling with a signing bonus of $4,000 when he was seventeen years old. He reached the major leagues after two seasons of minor league ball, the second of which was a stellar campaign with Visalia in the California League, where Pinson batted .367 with 20 home runs, 97 runs batted in, and 209 hits. He struggled in his first shot with the Reds in 1958 and eventually found himself back in the minor leagues before being called up to "the show" for good that September.

In 1959, Pinson's first full season in Cincinnati, he hit .316 with 20 home runs, 21 stolen bases, and 205 hits. He led the National League in runs scored (131) and doubles (47) and was named to that summer's National League All-Star team.

In 1963, Pinson was involved in an incident that some believe later undermined his support in the annual Hall of Fame vote conducted among baseball writers. *Cincinnati Post* sportswriter Earl Lawson opined in print on September 3 that Pinson "would hit .350 if he would only bunt once in a while instead of going for homers." The criticism angered Pinson, and he took a swing at Lawson who, in turn, had Pinson arrested. A trial resulted in a hung jury, and Lawson subsequently dropped the charges.

Despite debuting in the big leagues more than a decade after Jackie Robinson broke Major League Baseball's color barrier, Pinson, an African American, had to deal with his share of racism, particularly in the early stages of his career. He was close friends with his African American teammate, Frank Robinson, the 1961 National League Most Valuable Player and future Hall of Famer. Later, writing in his autobiography, Robinson reported that some writers viewed the two of them to be a "Negro clique," the price to be paid for two African American athletes being close friends in the 1960s.

Pinson suffered a stroke on October 5, 1995, and died sixteen days later at the age of fifty-seven.

◆

Vada Pinson III, born in 1963, grew up on Malcolm Avenue in Oakland, California, the only boy among four children.

"Both my parents were from Oakland. My grandfather was a longshoreman there, but our family was originally from Tennessee. We still have a big family back there. When my dad played with the Reds, we'd go [to Cincinnati] in the summertime and then we'd come back home and go to school. And then he got traded to St. Louis and we did the same thing there, and with each team he played for. So, we got to do a little bit of traveling during the summertime to be with him and watch him play and, you know, it was kind of fun because you meet a lot of different people."

Vada III attended a small Catholic school. When he was in the first grade, it was announced that his dad would be coming to the school to speak.

"The kids would always say, 'When is your dad coming?' I was a real shy kid and I got really nervous when my dad came to speak. He kind of put his hand around my shoulder and walked me up there. I was nervous. Everybody flocked to him and at a certain point, I was kind of left by myself. Dad came over and said, 'Just stay by my side, so I know where you're at.'"

Young Vada said he tried to block out his father's fame at that stage, to no avail.

"I really couldn't because a lot of people were like, 'Is your dad going to be our coach?' I started playing baseball, I think, in the fourth grade. It was a good experience for me because it brought me out of my shyness. It was like with my dad. I always thought of him as a shy person, but it's like he changed when he got around all these people. He became this other person and was very likable, signing autographs and giving advice to young players.

"So, it was fun in a way, but in some ways, it wasn't because, like, one of the guys, when I was growing up, would always say, 'Well, you're just getting "that" because your father is a baseball player.' I got a lot of that, but my mom and dad said just don't pay attention to it. They said to let it go over my head and to not get into fights."

Vada III was somewhat sheltered from racism when he was growing up, but it was there, nonetheless.

"My parents did a really good job of hiding it from me because I really didn't notice anything going on. But I remember one time I was in the car with [my father] and he said that if he never played baseball, he probably wouldn't be treated [as well as] he gets treated.

"But my mom was really good at giving me information on that. She said that after her first year in Cincinnati, she didn't want to return. She said the players would not speak to them, and the wives would not speak to them. She would always say that the tension was very high when they first started. My dad wanted to move to Cincinnati. My mother was like, 'No, no, we're not moving to Cincinnati!' She said that when he was on the road, she just didn't feel comfortable in the home."

Things apparently changed over time, though.

"The majority of our neighborhood was white, and our neighbors were the nicest people. I think the reason my dad loved living there was that nobody really bothered him about coming to get autographs.

"A while back I spoke to a woman who said her husband used to deliver water to our house a long time ago. I remembered that we used to have water delivered to the house and my mom used to yell at me 'cause I used to just open the door for anybody. Anyway, I went and met them for lunch, and I gave the man one of my dad's bobbleheads. And the guy actually started crying. It was so interesting to hear about his friendship with my father, where he would just come over and my father would invite him in and let him sit and talk with him in the house."

When his mom yelled at her son, it was probably "Manny" that she was chastising.

"My family calls me Manny instead of Vada because, one holiday season, my father and grandfather were there for Christmas dinner. And every time someone called 'Vada,' I'd come running in. So, they said, 'We're gonna have to think of another name for you,' so my mother came up with Manny. If you're around my family, that's what they call me."

Young "Manny" gave baseball a shot as a kid but ran into some obstacles.

"When I was young, I liked to play all sports. My best sport was probably basketball, but I didn't grow. My father was like 5-11, but I only grew to 5-9. Playing baseball for me was really difficult because a lot of people would say, 'Vada Pinson's son, Vada Pinson's son.' But I still loved to play the game. I was one of the best players on the team, but my father never actually showed me how to hit or throw a baseball. When he came to one of my first games, he asked me who taught me to do all that. I said I just watch television, and I'll watch you at your games, and I picked it up pretty good.

"I just felt that there was too much pressure at a certain point. I just felt that it didn't come to me the way I wanted it to."

The elder Pinson's baseball career didn't end in storybook fashion, either. He had harbored hopes of managing in the major leagues but never was given the opportunity.

"I don't think my dad was bitter, but it is something he always wanted to do. I remember the day after he passed, I went to his house, and he had all these baseball charts up. He had been let go by the Marlins (as a coach) at that point, and it was kind of like a very sad ending. The house was a sight. It looked like he was depressed; the house was full of stuff. It's like he just didn't care anymore. He had ribs in his freezer. So, I took them home—remember, this was 1995—and saw that the expiration date on the meat was 1986."

A seminal development in young Vada's life occurred when his parents divorced.

"Their divorce was really, really hard on me. I was in the fourth grade when it happened. And my father, at that point, just stopped coming around. I remember the day when he told everyone. But I had basketball practice, so I really wasn't worried about it. I was a kid, and I just ran out of the house. And Dad said he would talk to me, but I really felt like my dad did not come back and tell me why. My sister told me, 'Well, Mom and Dad aren't going to be together.' I said, 'What do you mean they're not going to be together anymore?' I didn't really understand the situation.

"But I think they made the final decision to divorce when my mother hit my father and he pushed her back to get her off of him. And my mom fell back, and she dislocated her shoulder. And then my dad pushed me, and I fell down the stairs. And it was over something that was not really making too much sense to me. And I just remember staying in my room and everybody was really, really quiet."

Young Vada found some solace by playing baseball, at least up to a point.

"So, I played baseball all the way up to possibly the ninth grade. And I was really good. There was a point where St. Mary's High School came and looked at me. But my mom asked me, 'Do you really want to keep going to Catholic school? You've been going to Catholic school all your life.' And I told her I would like to, but I think my mom and dad had a little falling out over the money. So she said, 'Well, why don't you try public school?' That was a big switch for me.

"My mother also wanted me to stick with one team. She didn't want me to [play] for a whole bunch of different teams because she wanted me to do my schoolwork. Another baseball player, Bip Roberts, grew up near me. We went running one day and he said it might be tougher for me [to have a career in baseball] because I only played for one team. He said, 'If they haven't seen you play, even though you're Vada's son, it might be difficult.'"

Most difficult of all, though, was the absence of Vada's father.

"When I graduated high school, he never reached out. And I was always wondering, did I do something wrong? And my mom's like, 'No, you didn't do nothing wrong. It's your father.'"

Before the divorce, his father was "always around," and the two sometimes took trips together.

"One time, during the off-season, he took me down to Fresno. Just me and him. He was doing a baseball clinic. I remember that was one of the first times I realized my dad was a big ballplayer. I remember my dad saying, 'Stay close, stay close, because there's going to be a lot of people.'"

Another moment that sticks in Vada III's mind is "The Bazooka Incident."

"In the clubhouse in Cincinnati, they had all these snacks and Bazooka gum. My sister said to make sure I brought some gum out for her. So, I filled up my pockets and put it in my socks and everything. And there was no gum left. And Frank [Robinson] walks in and says, 'Where's the Bazooka gum?' Frank came over. He picked me up and all the gum fell out [laughs]."

Young Vada joined the military after high school.

"When I joined the military, I wrote my dad a nice, long letter. I said, 'My baseball career, it's a wrap. I'm not going to try and play baseball anymore.'

"So, I'm in the service. And, lo and behold, my first year in the military, as soon as I got to Germany, guess who I get a letter from? My father. And it was a nice, long letter. It was right when the [Persian Gulf] war started, and he said that he wasn't able to sleep. He was worried about me. So, it kind of made me feel really, really good. I held onto that letter. I still have it. My father wasn't really good about showing compassion to us kids."

A bit later, after the war, there was an Associated Press article in *Stars & Stripes*. Headlined "Pinson glad son survived," the senior Pinson, then a coach with the Detroit Tigers, said, "He's doing a great job over there and I'm very proud of him." The article went on to quote father Pinson recounting his drive down to spring training in Lakeland, Florida:

> "I was always changing the dials on the radio to hear the latest news on the war. Doing that and thinking about my son so much—before I knew it, I was here. I've never watched more news shows on television in my life than I have lately. I wish I could change places with him because I've lived my life," said the 52-year-old Pinson. "He's just getting started."

But there's more to the story.

"You would not believe the pain that I got from that article. I went into a tent in another platoon. And there was a gentleman in that tent, and he really blew it out of proportion. He said to me, 'I don't give an eff who you are.' And one of my buddies came into the tent and got into it with him. Tensions were high. People were stressed. And my buddy took a swing at this guy and they had to be separated.

"And I'm like, 'How did this even happen?' Because I didn't tell anybody who my father was. Only select people would know because they would come up to me and ask. But they didn't make a big deal about it. I just wanted to be known as a hard worker and a good soldier. But that one incident made me want to get out of the service. Just that one incident, because the guy wanted to kill me. I loved my military service and until that point, I thought I was going to be a career soldier."

After the war, Vada saw his father for the first time at the wedding of young Vada's sister in 1992 or 1993.

"I saw him during the wedding, but he didn't have much to say. I actually had to go up to him and speak to him. I was in my military uniform. We sat and talked for a little while, and then that was it. I think the next time I saw my dad was when I was riding the bus and actually saw his car pull up alongside and I saw him in the car. And I was like, 'Wow, my dad is back in town.'"

Earlier in his life, Vada missed having another man around the house.

"I really, really, really, really struggled living with women [his mom and three sisters]. I ran away from home one time. I went to my grandparents', my father's parents', house. And I told them, 'I don't want to live with my mom anymore. I need to be around a man. I want to live with my father.' So, they called my father. And he said he couldn't take me at that point. I think I was in high school. He asked me what was wrong, and I said I was really struggling because all my friends are no longer my friends because now I'm going to public school, and I don't have anybody that I can really count on. 'I just wanna become a man. I need somebody to show me the way.'

"But he said he can't take me because he's traveling and everything. And I remember they took me back home to my house. And I was crying my eyes out."

That's when Vada decided to join the military.

"I said I'm just going to join the service and try to get away. And that's when I wrote the letter to my father. But after my sister's wedding, I just stopped trying to reach out because I felt he wasn't doing anything but hurting me."

The next time his father entered "Manny's" life was when he received a phone call from his sister saying that their dad was in the hospital.

"She said, 'Can you please come?' So, I left work and went to the hospital. And they said he had a stroke. He never regained consciousness the whole time he was in the hospital. The doctors said he probably had the stroke a couple of nights before. I think they said he had been home for like three days and nobody was able to reach him. He had tons of voicemails, so that's how we know he had been there for a while.

"My sister asked me why I was going to the hospital every day to see him; he really wasn't a good father. And I was, like, 'Because he's our father, and you know, you want somebody there to be with him.'

"I remember he was admitted October the fifth and my birthday was on the sixth. I was just praying that he didn't pass away on my birthday. He passed away on October 21. The one thing that I really wanted from him was just to hear him say, 'I love you.' The doctor said, 'You know, he probably can hear you.' So, I told [my father], if you hear me, say 'I love you,' squeeze my hand twice. And he did squeeze my hand twice."

Young Vada and his father were not close after the divorce, but in the years since the elder Vada's death, Pinson says he has gotten closer to his father through interactions with strangers. The water delivery man was one example, but there are many others.

"I stop by my father's grave sometimes. One time, a gentleman was sitting there. He said, 'Are you one of Vada's kids?' I said yes, and he said, 'Your father meant so much to me because he took time out for me when I was a kid.' And the guy started crying. I had one of my dad's baseball gloves in the back of my car and I gave it to him.

Vada Pinson III gets a uniform fitting from his dad as sister Renee looks on. *Vada Pinson III*

"Another gentleman flew in to go to my father's graveside. He had a Vada Pinson shirt.

"So, it's interesting because he touched so many people's lives. You would not believe how many Vadas I have on my [Facebook] page. And one of the things that's crazy is that there was this football player for Michigan named Vada Murray. He passed away at the age of thirty-two [editor's note: Murray was forty-three when he died of lung cancer in 2011]. I didn't even know that he was named [after my father]. His daughter was doing an interview on the news and said he was named after the famous baseball player."

Sometimes, it's hard for Vada III to reconcile the father he knew with the man known by the public.

"It leaves you kind of wondering like, well, I was his son. Why did he treat me this way? You know, you wish things, but you don't get it, you know, in regards to how you want your family to be. And I've always thought about it, you know. My mother was really good at taking pictures of us when we were children. When I look at the pictures, I look at the way my father is looking at me as a child. It looked like he was admiring me. There's a picture when he's showing me off, I guess, to Hank Aaron. It's like, 'This is my son.' When I see the picture, I'm like, where did we go wrong after that, you know?"

8

Yogi Berra and Larry Berra

Fielding Fungoes from Mickey Mantle

Lawrence Peter "Yogi" Berra was an American icon whose fame extended far beyond baseball. Count him among the few American athletes for whom one name, Yogi, is all it takes to generate recognition across the generations.

There are, of course, the great "Yogi-isms," like: "No one goes there anymore, it's too crowded"; "It gets late early out there"; "A nickel ain't worth a dime anymore"; and, perhaps the most enduring of all, "It ain't over till it's over."

But to reduce Yogi Berra to his colorful quotes is to grossly minimize the man's accomplishments both on and off the field.

The St. Louis–born Berra was an eighteen-time all-star catcher over the course of a playing career with the New York Yankees that ran from 1946 to 1963, plus a very brief comeback with the New York Mets in 1965. He won ten World Series championships as a player, the most of anyone in history, and another three as a coach. In all, he played, managed, and coached in twenty-one different World Series. Let that sink in for a moment: twenty-one World Series!

He was a three-time American League Most Valuable Player and led the powerful Yankees in runs batted in every season from 1949 to 1955, years when his teammates included the likes of Joe DiMaggio and Mickey Mantle.

He managed the Yankees to the World Series in 1964 on the strength of a strong September but shockingly was fired after the World Series loss to the St. Louis Cardinals in seven games. It was said at the time that he couldn't discipline the players, most of whom had been his teammates, but that ignored the fact that the team came off the mat in September and ultimately fell just one game short of being World Champions.

The Mets quickly hired Berra as a coach, and he later became their manager in 1972 following the sudden death of Gil Hodges. Berra managed the team to the 1973 World Series.

He returned to the Yankees as their manager in 1984. The following year, the Yankees started the season 6–10 and he was fired. This led to a falling out between Berra and the Yankees, one that wasn't resolved until team owner George Steinbrenner apologized to Berra in 1999.

Berra was inducted into baseball's Hall of Fame in Cooperstown, New York, in 1972. His uniform number 8 was retired by the Yankees that same year.

Less known to many are Berra's off-the-field heroics. He served as a gunner's mate at the Normandy landing during World War II, earning a Purple Heart, a Distinguished Unit Citation, two battle stars, and a European Theatre of Operations ribbon during the war, and the Navy's Lone Sailor Award in 2009, presented to Berra for exemplifying the Navy's core values. In 2015, he was posthumously awarded the Presidential Medal of Freedom by President Barack Obama. In 2021, a postage stamp in his honor was released by the US Postal Service, the first "single issuance" honoring a baseball player since a stamp of Lou Gehrig was released in 1989.

Berra and his wife, Carmen, had three sons, each of whom became pro athletes. Larry, the oldest, was a catcher in the Mets minor league system. Dale was a shortstop for the Pittsburgh Pirates, Yankees, and Houston Astros for eleven seasons, and Tim was a wide receiver for the Baltimore Colts in 1974.

Yogi Berra died in 2015 at the age of ninety. His legacy lives on in the form of the Yogi Berra Museum and Learning Center, which opened its doors in 1998 on the campus of Montclair State University in Little Falls, New Jersey. The museum promotes the values of respect and sportsmanship and conducts a wide range of school and public programs. Much of Berra's memorabilia is on display, along with other baseball artifacts. Adjacent to the museum is Yogi Berra Stadium, home of Montclair State's baseball team and, until the end of the 2022 season, the New Jersey Jackals of the independent Frontier League.

◆

Larry Berra entered the world in St. Louis on December 8, 1949. His dad was already an established major leaguer at that point, but it wasn't until several years later that Larry began to fully understand his dad's place in the baseball universe.

"I was fourteen when Dad became manager of the Yankees in 1964. And when he got fired, I was at a school called Montclair Academy. The whole place went into turmoil. They thought we were going to kill ourselves or were going to go crazy. But, of course, we didn't. But I'll tell you what, I don't know if I could have grown up if my father was playing now. Back then, we were in the community all the time. We had no problem going out. We weren't afraid of anything. He just taught us to be careful."

The Berras moved from St. Louis to Woodcliff Lake, New Jersey, when Larry was two. A few years later, the family moved to Tenafly, New Jersey, before settling in on Sutherland Road in Montclair in 1959.

"We were always out in the streets, playing ball. My mother was the den mother of my Cub Scout group. My father actually went to den meetings. He would go when we had boxcar races; he would come to our basketball games. He was just part of the community, and no one ever bothered him at all."

In those early years in Montclair, day baseball was still the norm in the major leagues.

"My father was almost always home for dinner" when the Yankees played at home. "He would spend as much time as he could with us. He didn't like to travel. He was a big family man. We went to the ballpark with him on the weekends. We were allowed to go in the clubhouse and run around on the field during batting practice. They didn't have all these insurance rules and everything else. It was like one big playground. And Sundays were like a family day out. My mother took us to both games of doubleheaders. We would take the bus in and then ride home with Dad. When the Yankees were home, we had this ritual. Monday nights, we would always eat at this one particular restaurant, a burger place that we loved."

Growing up, Larry considered the Yankees to be his extended family.

"I was friends with Gil McDougald's kids and Whitey Ford's kids, and also Charlie Silvera's and Hank Bauer's. I grew up with all of them. And spring training was our big thing because we were always together.

"One day I asked my dad if he could hit us some fly balls and he goes, 'Man, I'm too tired, ask Mickey.' So, here we are having Mickey Mantle hitting us fly balls. Can you imagine?"

When Carmen was pregnant with Larry, Yogi took an off-season job as a Sears hardware salesman to make some extra money. Needless to say, free agency was at best a dream in the 1950s.

"After he won his first MVP in '51, he started going on the banquet tour circuit during the winter, which at that time would pay maybe fifty or seventy-five bucks. He did quite a few of those for the Elks, the Lions Club, Rotary Clubs. And when I got to be five or six, he would take me with him to these things.

"But his whole philosophy of money was, 'I want my kids to go to school, I want my home, and I want to belong to a country club.' That's all he cared about. I mean, we're talking about a man who could have any car he wanted but he drove Corvairs and Ford Escorts and Pintos until he was sixty years old. He got a Jaguar from my mother for his sixtieth birthday, and at first, he wanted to turn it back in [laughs]."

Around the house, mom was the disciplinarian, but Dad had "the look."

"We always knew that if things got tough, you had to watch out. My father only spanked me once, and I knew that I never wanted it to happen again. You could always tell when something was annoying him by the way he looked."

One of the great life lessons Yogi instilled in his boys was about winning and losing.

"He taught us how to play gin, poker, and checkers. And one thing he never did was, he would never let us win. We had to beat him. He taught us how to win and lose. He'd say, 'Do you know why you lost? Remember that.'"

Apart from baseball, for a generation of kids, the name Yogi Berra is synonymous with the chocolate-flavored drink Yoo-Hoo. Berra was a spokesman and stockholder in the company.

"We used to do the Yoo-Hoo things on the weekends. I'd go with him. I was in tons of Two Guys, ShopRites, and A&Ps. Later, when I was going to Montclair High School, I went out for the baseball team in 1967. And the players all said, 'You're not getting on this team unless you bring a supply of Yoo-Hoo for every practice.' So, I drove down to the plant in New Jersey, loaded up the truck, and came back. I said, 'Is this enough?'"

Kidding aside, what was it like being the son of a baseball legend and having to try out for the high school baseball team?

"I thought I was going to be a bowler. I loved bowling and won two tournaments. My dad and Phil Rizzuto had a bowling alley in Clifton, New Jersey, and Dad would take me down there and I learned to bowl. My first job was there. I made a quarter an hour taking bowling balls off the racks. And then I thought I'd be a basketball player because when I was thirteen, I was already like 5-10. And I thought that when I was eighteen, I would be like, 6-4, 240. I made the 240 but peaked at 5-11 [laughs]. So, I started playing baseball at Montclair Academy. One night, when I was a freshman, I got a call from the coach saying, 'Have you ever caught?' I said, 'Not really, only in Little League.' And he said he needed me to catch because our catcher got the measles. So, I caught the next game and every game after that. I loved it.

"When I was playing in the Appalachian League, in Marion, Virginia, we went to one town, and I was in the on-deck circle. Some guy kept yelling at me, saying, 'You're not as good as your old man.' And I turned around and I said, 'Listen, if I was as good as my father, I wouldn't have to listen to you and I wouldn't be in this little town of yours.' And I got yelled at by my coach."

Larry's professional baseball career was short-lived, primarily because of injuries.

"I got hurt in the minor leagues, and unfortunately at that time, they cut you to pieces. They didn't have microsurgery like today. I had my first surgery, and it hampered me. My hitting went way down because I couldn't stride on my left leg. I'd fall over. I couldn't keep my balance, but I kept trying to play.

"Whitey Herzog was director of minor league development for the Mets. I said to him, 'You gotta do me a favor. If I'm not meeting your standards, you gotta let me go.' Everybody writes that I was released, but I was released because I asked them, not because they didn't think I could do it. I was very disappointed that I couldn't fulfill one of my dreams. I probably should have signed [a contract] out of high school but my mother wanted me to go to college."

Larry says his baseball acumen came mostly from observation, putting into practice one of his dad's classic comments: "You can observe a lot by just watching." But his dad did give Larry a piece of useful baseball advice when he was in college.

"I came home one day and I asked if he could watch me swing the bat. He goes, 'Show me your stance.' So, he looks at me and he goes, 'Your hands are too close to your body, put them back a little bit.' And I went four for seven the next day against Rutgers."

Another time, "He helped me on throwing the ball to second base. I asked him one night how to adjust my feet. And that was it. Everything else, I picked up by watching or listening to players talk. When I'd ask my dad to play catch, he would go, 'That's what you have brothers for.'

"My brother Tim and I used to play Wiffle Ball in the backyard. We had a big area back there. We'd wrap the Wiffle Ball in black electric tape so we could really throw it hard. Tim had a really good arm. One day Dad comes home and says, 'Give me the bat.' Tim threw one pitch and Dad hit the ball over the backyard, over the swimming pool, and into the neighbor's backyard."

Mention of the Berras' swimming pool conjures up for Larry an indelible image from his youth.

"Sometimes, [Dad] would come home and he would vacuum the swimming pool. He would put his bathing suit on. With his body in a bathing suit, he was hysterical."

Larry has six children, four boys and two girls.

"Dad was the best grandpa. He'd go to all their hockey games, all their basketball games, a lot of their baseball games. He'd sit out in right field or somewhere because one thing he hated [if he's watching a game] was people bothering him during the time of play. He would always tell people to come by at halftime or between periods."

Berra family members went to the Obama White House in November 2015 to accept the Presidential Medal of Freedom on behalf of their father, who died just two months earlier.

"I'm a very patriotic guy. I went with Lindsay [Larry's daughter] and my brothers to accept the medal and the feeling was just amazing. I got to meet the president of the United States and his wife and the way they treated us down there, it was amazing and fabulous.

He got the medal along with Willie Mays, Gloria Estefan, Barbra Streisand, and a bunch of other people. I know Dad would have said, 'Why am I with these people? I'm not that important.' We used to tell him, 'You don't realize the effect that you have on people and what you mean to them.'"

Like most vets, Yogi Berra didn't speak much about his wartime efforts.

"He would tell you that he was in the Navy. He would tell you he was at D-Day and that was about it. When the movie *Saving Private Ryan* came out, we went together. When the movie was over, you could see that he was visibly upset. I said, 'What's the matter?' And he goes, 'That brought back something.' Because, you know, he was that close. He was three hundred yards, four hundred yards off-shore, and he was firing machine guns and rockets before the soldiers went onto the beach. The day after that he had the job of taking the bodies out of the water. And that hit him hard. He told us they were bloated and how much he did not like doing that, but it was his job. And that's basically the only time he ever started talking about it."

For all that Yogi Berra accomplished, it seems surprising that a movie had never been made of his life until the documentary *It Ain't Over,* which premiered at the 2022 Tribeca Film Festival. Larry offers a theory as to why it took so long for his dad's life to be portrayed on-screen.

"Everybody wants to see turmoil or some kind of conflict or something like that. And there never really was any, family-wise. My father was always taking care of his family, you know, whatever they needed. He'd help both sides. And my mother and father were married for sixty-five years. They just knew how to do it. My mother was a huge part of my father's life. They were basically inseparable. The only thing that kept them apart was golf. He loved his golf. But it was an incredible romance."

Yogi Berra reads a bedtime story to Larry. Notice the sports-themed curtains, perhaps a decorating suggestion from babysitter Martha Kostyra, aka Martha Stewart. *Yogi Berra Museum and Learning Center*

There was, however, one very public conflict, the cold war between Yogi Berra and the Yankees that lasted from 1985 to 1999.

"That conflict could have been over quickly. All George [Steinbrenner] had to do was to apologize to him. My father never said a bad word about George. He just said, 'The man lied to me.' He had many guys call him to say George wants to apologize. And he would always say, 'Tell George to call me himself.' And as soon as George apologized, it was like it never happened. But it was fourteen years later; that was the problem."

Larry tells one final Yogi Berra story in a life that was overflowing with them:

"My father's brother moved from St. Louis to Bloomfield, New Jersey, to run the bowling alley. He ran lounges and bartended in St. Louis. So, my father brought him east to work at the bowling alley and later he moved to Nutley, New Jersey. And sometimes we would go over to my aunt and uncle's house, and the parents would go out and this blonde girl from Nutley would come over to babysit us."

The girl's name was Martha Kostyra. The world now knows her as Martha Stewart.

"We basically never realized it until my mother was at a charity event in New York City one day. And Martha Stewart came up to her and said, 'How's Larry doing?' My mom said, 'How do you know my son?' Martha said, 'Because I used to babysit him in Nutley for John and Betty Berra.' My mother was like, 'Oh, my goodness.'"

Today, Larry Berra is president and owner of a New Jersey–based company that makes OSHA, FDA, and USDA-compliant flooring for research laboratories and pharmaceutical plants. The company's name? Diamond 8 Flooring . . . another tip of the cap to Dad.

Dave McNally and Jeff McNally

A National Television Debut at Age Seven

For baseball fans in the late 1960s and early 1970s, Baltimore Orioles pitcher Dave McNally was a visitor in their living rooms pretty much every October. From 1966 to 1974, the 5-11, 185-pound left-hander pitched in five separate American League Championship Series and four World Series. In all, he pitched in fourteen post-season games (twelve starts) during that nine-year stretch, throwing 90.1 innings.

McNally made a loud major league debut with Baltimore on September 26, 1962, hurling a two-hit shutout versus the Kansas City Athletics at the age of nineteen. By the time his career ended at the age of thirty-two in 1975, McNally had compiled a stellar 184–119 won-lost record (.607 winning percentage), with numerous highlights along the way.

He won twenty or more games in four consecutive seasons (1968–1971), including a league-leading twenty-four wins in 1970, and received Most Valuable Player and Cy Young Award votes during each of those four years. He became part of history in 1971 when he and Orioles teammates Jim Palmer, Mike Cuellar, and Pat Dobson each were twenty-game winners, the last time a pitching staff accomplished this feat (and, given the way starting pitchers are now deployed, likely never to be replicated). The three-time all-star threw two-hundred-plus innings eight times. In 1969, he captivated the baseball world by starting the season 15–0.

And then there are McNally's World Series exploits, both on the mound and at the plate. He was 4–2 in World Series play, including a four-hit shutout in game four of the 1966 series, completing Baltimore's sweep of the Los Angeles Dodgers and giving the Birds their first-ever world championship.

In the 1970 World Series versus the Cincinnati Reds, he pitched a complete game to win game three, but the big story is what he did at the plate. In the bottom of the sixth inning, McNally hit a grand slam off pitcher Wayne Granger, becoming the first—and only—pitcher to hit a bases-loaded home run in the World Series. McNally also hit a two-run homer in the 1969 World Series, making him and Hall of Famer Bob Gibson the only pitchers to ever hit two career home runs in the Fall Classic.

Interestingly, McNally was at best a mediocre hitting pitcher, compiling a .133 career batting average in the regular season. He did hit nine regular-season home runs, but it took him 848 plate appearances to do so, or one per 94 at-bats. In the World Series, though, he managed to hit two out of the park in only 28 plate appearances. So, with apologies to Reggie Jackson, McNally's fans and teammates rightfully could have considered him to be "Mr. October" at the plate.

Off the field, the Billings, Montana, native was known as a tough contract negotiator in the pre-free-agency era, when players had very little bargaining leverage. McNally, in fact, was instrumental in helping to bring about free agency in baseball, which exponentially elevated player salaries throughout the major leagues.

Before the 1975 season, Baltimore traded McNally to the Montreal Expos. He never signed a contract and instead had his 1974 Baltimore deal renewed by the team, as was their right at the time under the collective bargaining agreement between the team owners and the players union. In June 1975, McNally retired but, at the urging of Marvin Miller, executive director of the union, did not formally file retirement papers with the league. Miller asked McNally to join pitcher Andy Messersmith, who also pitched the 1975 season under a team-renewed contract, in suing to overturn baseball's reserve clause, which essentially bound players to a team for life, or until the team decided to trade or release the player. McNally agreed, and an arbitrator later ruled in favor of their argument that they had played out their "option year" and were now entitled to shop their services to other teams. Messersmith signed a free agent deal with the Atlanta Braves following the ruling. McNally remained retired.

In 1978, McNally was inducted into the Orioles Hall of Fame, the first pitcher to be so honored and the third player overall, following Frank and Brooks Robinson. In 2000, *Sports Illustrated* magazine named McNally Montana's Athlete of the Century.

McNally died of cancer in Billings on December 1, 2002. He was sixty years old.

◆

Jeff McNally is the oldest of five children, three girls flanked by two boys, born to Dave and Jean McNally. Jeff was born during spring training in 1963, with his dad hoping to break camp with the major league club for the first time.

"[Dad] was in Florida for spring training. When I was about due, mom went back to Billings to be with her family when I was born. And then we moved to Baltimore."

Jeff grew up in Baltimore, but the family maintained close ties to Billings.

"We stayed in Baltimore year-round and went back to Billings every summer and visited. We lived in the row houses in downtown Baltimore for the first few years. We lived right around the corner from the Powells [Orioles teammate Boog Powell and his family, including son John W. Powell]. I have this very vivid memory of those little fire trucks with pedals. [JW and I] were two or three years old or whatever. And we used to meet out on the sidewalk. We each had one of those things and we kind of tooled around on them. We lived there maybe three years, then we moved to the Lutherville-Timonium area, just north of downtown Baltimore. And we lived there from like '66 to '75, when [Dad] retired.

"We had a great neighborhood. We lived in a development in the suburbs, just kind of classic suburban life. The neighborhood we were in had been a farm. Right next to our development was a big cornfield that we used to love to rummage through and, you know, make a fort in there. We'd get in trouble from the farmer 'cause we didn't know what we were doing, but we're like killing his corn by rolling around, forming forts and trails and things like that. But there were also some big, open lots that we played baseball on, and that was really fun."

Jeff got to spend a considerable amount of time with his dad during the off-season.

"During the off-season, he was around a lot. The owner of the Orioles back then [Jerold Hoffberger] owned a brewery. And so, some of the players worked in the off-season for the brewery. I can remember [Dad] heading off to work a few times. He did sales or something, but that was just for maybe one or two winters. [In later off-seasons], a group of the players would work out at the YMCA; that's where they did their off-season training. Probably in those old, gray sweats, you know? They also put together a basketball team for about nine or ten [players] as a way of doing off-season training."

During the season, Jeff got to spend plenty of time at the ballpark.

"My mom took me to most of the games, even when I was pretty young. As I got older, I was able to do things like spend some time in the locker room after games or whatever and kind of have a more fun experience with it. There was a section in the stands where the players' families had tickets. And I just remember that feeling of being around all those wives and kids and it was a really fun experience."

Jeff McNally sheds tears (of joy?) at spring training with his dad in 1964. *Jeff McNally*

Jeff describes being in the locker room as a bit overwhelming.

"Compared to these days, the locker rooms were nothing, you know? But I remember just being really impressed. The smell of the leather, the tables of food and drinks and stuff, and they're just spread out around the room. I remember, I must've been older, like 11 or 12, and my dad wanted to show off how I could throw. He gave me this wadded-up thing, like a ball of tape shaped like a baseball, and said, 'Okay, throw and hit the garbage can over there in the corner.' I remember feeling like extreme pressure. And so, I threw it and not only hit the can, it went in the can! I remember feeling really proud that I was able to do that for my dad when he put himself out there.

"There was a group of [kids] that were about the same age. JW [Powell], the Robinson boys; Jim Palmer had a couple of girls that were about my age. We kind of hung out at the games. I remember a game where we were behind and the four or five of us were sitting together and decided to start a rally thing in the stands. We started a chant that got the whole stands going. And [the Orioles] came from behind from four or five runs to win. And we took total credit for that [laughs]."

Did fans know the chant was started by some of the players' kids?

"It was different back then, you know? Even these great players, they weren't the celebrities that they are now. People didn't quite look at the players and their families the same way they do now, which was kind of nice. I don't think [the other fans] knew who we were or paid attention to who that group was over there."

Jeff enjoyed a moment in the spotlight when his dad hit a grand slam in game six of the 1970 World Series. NBC sportscaster Tony Kubek interviewed Jeff and his mom in the stands the following inning. After posing a couple of questions to Jean McNally, Kubek turned to Jeff and the following conversation ensued:

Kubek: "Jeff, when your pops came up there with the bases loaded, what were you thinking about?"

Jeff [in a squeaky, seven-year-old voice]: "I thought he wasn't going to get a hit. I thought he was going to get out."

"I vividly remember it," Jeff says more than a half-century later. "I remember looking up and seeing that my dad was coming up to hit and, oh, crap, it's my dad. I decide it's too bad my dad's up because the bases are loaded and we're not going to be able to take advantage of it."

Jeff was dressed well for his national television debut, wearing a handsome plaid sports jacket.

"Back then, you dressed up for those games. Men had suits on, women had dresses. And so, my mom dressed me up. Oh yeah, I looked pretty sharp [laughs]."

Another fond memory for Jeff is that of tossing the ball around with his dad.

"He really hurt his arm badly in 1967 and missed a big chunk of that season. As '68 rolled around, he wasn't even being counted on [for] the [starting] rotation. He still really couldn't even throw. He tried one last-ditch effort to try and have it get better. And it worked. But his arm always kind of bothered him from there on out. And by the time he retired, it was just kind of trashed. But I remember playing catch with him, especially in high school. I was playing baseball and he was helping with our team and helping with me. And there was this, like, zip-pop when he threw the ball just playing catch, just this zip-pop and this little movement that I didn't appreciate at the time. But looking back now, I remember the way the ball kind of popped in my glove in a way that when I threw, it didn't. Even all those years after he retired and his arm was trashed, he still had this kind of natural pop and movement to the ball."

Jeff says there wasn't much baseball talk around the McNally household.

"He was a super competitive person. He loved it when he did it, but it wasn't what he wanted to talk about when he wasn't at work. We talked more about baseball after he retired. When I was in high school, we had a very good baseball program, the same one he played in high school. We had, like, a sixty-five-game schedule and we traveled all over the Northwest. [Dad] helped with our pitchers and helped our coach. We talked a lot about baseball when he coached, but it wasn't big around the kitchen table."

There is one lesson in particular that Jeff remembers.

"In my junior or senior year, I hit a really bad stretch with my hitting. I was really struggling. And he pulled me aside after one game and he was irritated. He didn't get super irritated very often with me, but he was really irritated because after I hit weak ground ball after weak ground ball, I guess I was cursing as I ran down the first base line, like, loud cursing that people could hear. He pulled me aside and said he didn't care if I was 0 for 20, that 'You don't do that. That is not cool. It's not a way to be a leader for your teammates. They don't need to see you being frustrated and doubting yourself. And people in the stands don't want to see that either. So, you need to knock that off.' [It was about] learning to be a good person and grow up and treat the game and people with respect."

But there were off-the-field lessons, too.

"I think [Dad] understood the business world maybe better than others [did]. He understood what was fair, and the unfair advantage owners had back then. He was thought of as being a hard negotiator; he wasn't afraid to stand up for what he thought was right. He talked a lot about how many amazing players the Orioles had in their minor league system that never got a chance to play in the majors because they had Brooks Robinson and Dave Johnson and Mark Belanger and all these players ahead of them. And so, they got stuck in the minors and he thought that was really unfair.

"I remember the whole thing with the Expos vividly because we had several family meetings around the decision, to agree to the trade [from Baltimore]. The only leverage you had back then as players was, if you were with the same team for ten years you could decline a trade. We talked as a family about Montreal and having to move and everything. And, you know, this is my father's version obviously, but they agreed on a contract, a gentleman's agreement or whatever. And so, he agreed to the trade and then, in his view, they reneged on [the agreement]. So, he refused to sign a contract. So, he started the season without a contract.

"His arm was just trashed, and he wasn't having a good experience, so like overnight he decided to retire. He just packed up and came home in the middle of the night. We didn't even know. There were no cell phones back then. He finished the game, packed up, got home like three in the morning, and said, 'I'm done.'

"It didn't take any convincing when they [the players' union] called him to join the lawsuit [challenging the reserve clause]. He really felt like it was the right thing to do. So, he was on board.

"There were a lot of interesting things that happened around that. I have the original letter the Expos' owner sent to [Dad] saying, basically, hey, why don't you pull out of this lawsuit thing and we'll have you sign a contract with this amount, with a bonus for this amount and you don't even have to necessarily come back and play, or you can show up for a day or whatever. It's all typed out and there's actually a handwritten [part]: 'If you want your wife to come with you, we will pay for that, too.' It's a fascinating piece of memorabilia."

Jeff, a third baseman and shortstop, was drafted out of high school by the Milwaukee Brewers but chose to enroll at Stanford University instead. Was he tempted to turn pro?

"I was because it sounded very romantic, you know? I really loved baseball. I lived and breathed baseball. [Turning pro] was appealing. But my dad was really good at this kind of thing. He knew, especially with an offer from Stanford, that it made no sense for me to sign a contract when I was eighteen and try to work my way through the minor leagues. He knew that no matter how talented you are, the chances of making it are slim. But he was great that way as a father because he would never say, 'You're not gonna do that, you're not going to sign with the Brewers.' He just sat down with me and we talked through what it would look like and what it would mean. It was obvious to me what he preferred, but he let me make the choice, which was really smart in hindsight because it was the right choice. I kept getting injured and having knee surgeries, but I had a great experience at Stanford and that kind of launched me into a lot of other things and friendships that I never would have had."

Jeff played baseball at Stanford but tore up his knee while cross-country skiing during Christmas vacation in his sophomore year.

"Back then, there were no scopes or anything. They just kind of opened you up and took everything out. I came back for the end of

that season, but I had a second surgery that summer after my sophomore year and decided I was just not going to play anymore and to
focus on my pre-med [studies]."

Today, Jeff is an MD. He is internal medicine boarded, later
practiced emergency room medicine for twenty-five years, and now
works in hospice medicine as senior medical director for Inter-
mountain Healthcare.

Dave McNally was diagnosed with cancer at age fifty-five.

"He passed the weekend of Thanksgiving in 2002. It was pretty
obvious on that Saturday that it was really close. My sister, who is
my next youngest sibling, just had her first baby like a week before
that or something. And they jumped on a plane and brought her
daughter [to Billings]. And he got a chance to meet her just before
he passed.

"At Thanksgiving, he had dinner at the table with everybody, but
by Friday he was really struggling. And my brother had this conversation with him, and it was the first time I knew of him ever saying,
'Well, you know, I kind of brought this on myself because I smoked
all those years.' It just breaks my heart to have him thinking something like that because they all smoked back then. I remember there
were cartons of cigarettes on the table, in the locker room. I guess he
had quit five years before he was diagnosed."

At his dad's funeral, Jeff gave what was described in the local press
as a particularly touching eulogy in which he cited his father's great
sense of humor. He cites an example:

"My mom sends out this picture to all of us every Easter just to
remind us of him. [He's wearing] an amazing bunny costume that
has a thing that goes around the head with these ears. I remember
the year he wore that. He was generally a pretty quiet, pragmatic
[guy], so when he would throw things in like that it was very funny."

The funeral was well attended, but not in an overwhelming sort
of way to the family.

"It was actually really nice. I remember the day of the funeral, driving over to the church. There were a lot of people. It was packed, a couple of media cameras parked out there, but nothing insane or intrusive. It felt more just like a recognition of somebody who was highly thought of in the community."

Jack Aker and Matt Aker

If It's Tuesday, This Must Be Lynchburg

If you want to stump your friends for fun or to make a quick buck, here's the question to ask: "Who holds the New York Yankees record for most consecutive scoreless innings pitched?"

You can show your sporting nature by allowing five guesses. Your friends will throw out names like Whitey Ford (he holds the World Series record for most consecutive scoreless innings), Ron Guidry, Roger Clemens, Gerrit Cole, Catfish Hunter, David Cone, Andy Pettitte, Mel Stottlemyre, Allie Reynolds, Vic Raschi, and Al Downing. They might even reach way back for names like Jack Chesbro, Red Ruffing, or Bob Shawkey.

After your friends have exhausted themselves with your mental rope-a-dope, you tell them the answer: Jack Aker.

And then they might say, "Who?"

Aker was a successful relief pitcher whose career spanned from 1964 to 1974. He debuted in the major leagues with the Kansas City A's and in 1966 was named American League "Fireman of the Year" when he compiled a then-record thirty-two saves to go along with a 1.99 ERA across 113 innings.

In October 1968, he was selected by the Seattle Pilots in the expansion draft for the 1969 season. On May 20, 1969, he was traded to the Yankees for pitcher Fred Talbot. And that's where the fun begins.

Aker made his Yankee debut on May 24, 1969, throwing a scoreless inning against the Minnesota Twins. On May 28, in his third game with the Bombers, Aker allowed one run against the Chicago White Sox in the sixth inning before recording the final out. And that was it for allowing runs in May. And June. And most of July. On July 29, Aker retired the first two batters in the bottom of the eighth inning at Oakland before allowing three runs in a 6–5 Yankees loss.

From the final out on May 28 through the first two outs on July 29, Aker threw thirty-four consecutive scoreless innings, a team record that still stands. If you prefer not to count the May 28 and July 29 games, when Aker was scored upon, the streak covers thirty-three consecutive scoreless innings over eighteen appearances.

Aside from his place in Yankees trivia history, Jack Aker can also lay claim to being the Zelig of baseball (Zelig was a Woody Allen-created character who unexpectedly kept turning up alongside famous people and events).

For example, Aker actually pitched in the same major league game as the legendary Satchel Paige. In 1965, A's owner Charley Finley staged a promotion where he signed the fifty-eight-year-old former Negro League great to a major league contract. Paige started one game for the A's and pitched three innings of one-run ball before taking a seat (specifically, a rocking chair) in the A's bullpen. Aker pitched the final inning of that game.

On July 20, 1969, Aker was on the mound at Yankee Stadium when public address announcer Bob Sheppard told the crowd that the Apollo 11 astronauts were about to land on the moon. Play stopped while the fans were kept informed of the crew's approach to the lunar surface.

On April 8, 1974, Aker was in the Atlanta Braves bullpen when one of his fellow relievers, Tom House, etched his name into the trivia books by catching the ball that Hank Aaron hit for his 715th career home run, the one that broke Babe Ruth's record.

Aker also saved the first win in the history of the Seattle Pilots franchise, a footnote to the team's one year in Seattle (they moved to Milwaukee and became the Brewers in 1970), a season famously chronicled in Jim Bouton's bestseller, *Ball Four.*

In addition to the A's, Yankees, Pilots, and Braves, Aker pitched for the Chicago Cubs and New York Mets before a bad back forced him to retire after the 1974 season.

He later managed in the minor leagues for the Mets and Cleveland Indians, and was an Indians coach in 1986 and 1987.

Having a Native American heritage, Aker ran baseball clinics for Native American youths, and for these efforts he was presented with a "Giant Steps Award" by President Bill Clinton.

◆

Matt Aker was born right after the 1969 season in which his dad compiled his record-setting consecutive scoreless innings streak. Matt quickly became as familiar with the moving van as he was with the family car.

"It's funny, you know, when it's going on at the time you don't think about [moving]. It seems normal. I made friends very easily because kids around the ballpark are all there basically for the same reason—they love baseball. There was a whole underbelly to minor league parks in the seventies and eighties. The kids rarely watched the games. We were running, playing behind the scenes. By the time I was eleven, twelve, thirteen, I wanted to be around the players more and learn more. So, I would sit in the bullpens. I became a batboy for two years so I could rotate to opposing teams' dugouts and things like that. For me, making friends wasn't really difficult because we were always moving to a new town where baseball was kind of the center focus of everything."

Listening to Matt Aker talk, it's hard not to think of Johnny Cash singing "I've Been Everywhere."

"For sixth grade, I went to like four schools and missed six weeks while we were in Puerto Rico for winter ball. Oh, and I loved Lynchburg [Virginia]. I started school in the first grade. I went there through fifth grade and that was the first time we had a house where we were kind of steady. During the off-season, when my dad was a Yankee, Cub, Met, and Brave, we lived in Baltimore because my mother's parents lived there and ran a technical trade school there. We lived in an apartment in Baltimore. During the season when Dad was with the Yankees we lived in Ridgewood, New Jersey."

Matt Aker's dad (right) introduces him to Atlanta Braves team-mate Hank Aaron. *Matt Aker*

Matt's parents divorced when he was twelve or thirteen years old, which led to additional relocations.

"Once I reached the age of fourteen, I felt a responsibility to live with my mother during the school year because I was with my father during the summer."

This arrangement impacted Matt's baseball development to a degree.

"When I was seventeen, they had this thing called the Big League World Series, which is very much like the Little League World Series. They'd bring in teams from everywhere and it's played in Broward [Florida] and there are scouts there. But I left at the halfway point of the season to go live with Dad. By the end of the season, I still had the home run lead for Broward County. But I didn't get to play in the All-Star game. I didn't play a summer-league season until my senior year when I played American Legion baseball."

Nonetheless, Matt harbored dreams of following his dad to the big leagues. Matt starred as a pitcher and infielder at Chaminade-Madonna College Prep High School in Hollywood, Florida, earning Broward County District 15-3A Athlete of the Year honors for baseball. He also was named *Miami Herald* Scholar-Athlete of the Year and *Fort Lauderdale Sun-Sentinel* Scholar-Athlete of the Year, and he represented Broward County in the state high school all-star game.

Matt had the advantage of having his dad as a personal coach.

"We would go to the ballpark early a lot of times. And he would catch bullpens for me, and he'd talk about release points and what I'm doing wrong here or there. But it was never negative. It was always very instructional and extremely competitive. I remember as a young hitter, hitting a ball really hard off Dad and then just watching it. And he'd say, 'Don't watch it, just get right back in and hit.' And I'd hit another ball hard and watch it. And he'd stick one in my back and he'd go, 'That's what's going to happen to you if you sit and watch.' Not in a mean way; he'd giggle and laugh about it.

"I played in the state all-star game with Alex Fernandez and some other guys who ended up playing in the big leagues. I felt that I had a shot. But I wasn't very big, about 6-1, 165 when I graduated high school. I went to Palm Beach Community College, and they had a bunch of infielders, so I ended up being needed to pitch. I think I had sixty-two appearances in two years there."

Matt says he went to community college because "it was free. One of my goals was to go somewhere and not have my parents incur the expense."

Of course, had his dad pitched in today's era, he would have made millions of dollars and money might have been less of a concern.

"Dad was 'Fireman of the Year' in '66. He set the major league record for saves and Charles Finley wanted to remain the same with [Dad's] salary. He was making virtually nothing. Dad held out and said, 'I'll leave baseball before I'll sign for this.' And Finley eventually gave him a small raise, but I think that sealed the deal for my dad in Kansas City or in Oakland [where the A's moved for the 1968 season]. Finley held a grudge about that."

Jack Aker pitched and managed in the days when most players needed to take off-season jobs just to make ends meet.

"When Dad was managing at Lynchburg, he worked as a carpenter. Dad would go in the mornings during the winter, and he would work as a carpenter in these old antebellum houses that this guy was renovating and flipping. When Dad was playing and we were living in Baltimore during the winter, he would work for Brooks Robinson's sporting goods company. That's why we went to Puerto Rico—winter ball actually paid better."

After community college, Matt enrolled at the University of Mississippi, Ole Miss, where he played under Jake Gibbs, a former Yankee teammate of Jack Aker's.

"I really fell in love with Ole Miss after my visit there. They had the newest stadium of anybody. I mean, we had tunnels underneath and locker rooms underneath with televisions; it was a major league locker room. I think that was in part attributable to Jake and what he learned in the Yankees organization about treating your players right."

An elbow injury midway through his senior year derailed Matt Aker's pro ball ambitions.

"Honestly, I don't know that I ever had the quality stuff to be a major league pitcher. One of the good things about traveling with your father throughout the minor leagues is that you get to see all sorts of professional players. One of the bad things is that it gives you a real sense of reality as to your limitations and abilities. I knew that professional baseball was extremely tough. One of the things that Dad did was he never dissuaded me or overly pumped me up. He says to this day that the biggest problem for me was that I knew the game too well because I could play infield and pitch. He feels like if I had just played infield and focused on getting bigger and stronger as a third baseman, that I could have had a pro career there. He also feels that if I just focused on pitching for my entire high school career, then maybe I would have developed more arm strength.

"I was always picking [Dad's] brain because you think baseball is going to be part of your life forever. There were a lot of interesting moments because at the end of every night, no matter where we were, whether we were at home or on the road, he had to pick up a phone and call an answering machine in New York. This was the age before computers. He would say, 'This is Jack Aker calling in for the Lynchburg Mets. The date is, we played so-and-so tonight. The final score was, blah, blah, blah. And then he would go into a step-by-step review of every player who played [in that game]. So, every night when I was on the road [with Dad] I would hear what it took to be a major league baseball player.

"And then, of course, the inevitable happens. You build a bond with a player and all of a sudden the next day Dad has to call him into the office and release him. There was a player that I really liked when [Dad] was managing in Buffalo. He was a tremendous guy. So,

I guess I was thirteen and I heard my dad say over the phone, 'He's a non-prospect, a great guy. He would be good in our organization possibly as a coach down the road.' And so, I knew that this guy, who worked really, really hard every day and was a great guy who would be smiling tomorrow, had no idea that his future had kind of been earmarked already in the organization."

When he was playing, Matt says, he felt more of an internal pressure to succeed, more so than feeling pressure because he was the son of a former major leaguer.

"The first year I played Kids Pitch baseball, my dad was only able to make one game. There was pressure because all season everybody had said, 'Oh, your dad's the manager at Lynchburg.' And I had a pretty decent season, nothing great. The one time he was able to come, I struck out four times. I felt like I had let him down. For me, there was that kind of pressure more than from outside people because, I guess, even at a young age I played better than a lot of the kids around me.

"But I felt the pressure at the end of my playing career. I was, like, how did I not end up a professional player, you know, with all this experience and my background? But it came down to one thing, and that was natural talent. I didn't throw ninety-five miles an hour, and I wasn't going to suddenly throw ninety-five miles an hour. So, that was a realization for me. That was probably the most disappointed I ever was."

But Matt did end up following in his dad's footsteps, as a coach.

"After I graduated from Ole Miss, I stayed there for a year and coached as a student assistant. I was able to work with the pitchers and the hitters. The head coach was Don Kessinger [a former major league shortstop] and he said, 'Have you ever thought about [coaching] high school? There's a high school right down the road that needs a coach. You could start today.' So, I ended up coaching there for seven years, came back to South Florida, coached three years down here in a private school, and then moved back to North Carolina to raise my children. And that's when I started college coaching again [at Greensboro College]."

Today, Matt is an English teacher at Martin County High School in Stuart, Florida, just north of Palm Beach. He also works as a baseball instructor for U.S. Sports Camps, whose title sponsor is Nike.

Teaching and coaching are major components of the Aker family DNA.

In addition to managing in the minor leagues and coaching for the Indians, Jack Aker devoted a couple of summers to providing free baseball instruction to at-risk Native American youths in New Mexico.

"He went out to the reservations. He said that none of the kids had [baseball] gloves. So, he made a couple of calls and got a bag of gloves sent there. Then he realized that the sand had these little plants with small burrs on them. And the baseball would get covered in these burrs. So, he made sure that they leveled the field and added dirt, and over the course of a couple of years, the facility got a little better to where the kids could actually enjoy the game. He really takes a lot of pride in that. He really takes pride in the fact that he gave back to the Native Americans."

Jack Aker is part Potawatomi Indian, hence his nickname, "Chief."

"Nowadays, you have to walk on eggshells whenever you say something like that but, honestly, it never offended any of us. We take it as a sign of respect. I'm actually on the tribal roster, as are my sons."

Jack's Native American heritage was "mostly on his grandmother's side," according to Matt. "She was full-blooded or half-blooded American Indian. His father was named Bill Cloud Thrasher Aker. Grandpa Bill was a farmer out in Visalia, California. Dad grew up on a farm. His entire childhood was out in the country. As a child, he had a pet bobcat, which is kind of unusual. He found it as a kitten in the Sierra Mountains. It was really a unique way to grow up."

Of course, Matt grew up in a unique way, too.

"From the time I was a child until I was eighteen, my summers were spent wherever Dad was coaching or playing. I went to the ballpark every day at 2:30 or 3 o'clock. And then I would spend the day, typically, in uniform. I was on the field, and I would shag and play catch with players before the game. I terrorized Lynchburg for five or six years as a child, running around the stadium and playing cup ball [a kids' game]. The game would end 10:30 or 11, and I'd meet Dad in the clubhouse and hang around until he did his interviews or talked with his players or whatever. And then we'd get in the car to go home, or on the bus to go to the hotel.

"I can still remember, when Dad was with the Yankees, I was two or three and I would run around the table when they would have cocktail parties and stuff like that. The [players and their families] would come and eat dinner at each other's house. I remember the players with their huge lapels would come into the house, and all the wives would always play with the kids. [Major league pitcher] Danny Frisella was a super friend of my dad's and my mom's. He died in a freak dune buggy accident. I remember my mother sitting and crying and the Frisellas coming to our house because their kids were the same age. I think families of the minor leaguers and major leaguers were much closer-knit back then. It was kind of a closed community; they were really close."

Matt recalls riding to Yankee Stadium with his dad when they lived in New Jersey during his years playing for the Yankees.

"He used to love the drives. The drive to the ballpark allowed him to focus before he got there. And the drive back was a decompression. But if I had questions, he always answered them.

"We never lived close to the ballparks, like when he was coaching in Cleveland we could have lived right near the stadium. I mean, he was making decent money then, but we lived on the other side in Erie so that he could drive the bridge. It gave him twenty or thirty minutes to decompress after the game so that when he walked in the house, it was all over."

One particularly unique summer occurred in 1984 when his dad was managing the Buffalo Bisons, a Cleveland Indians farm team.

"They filmed *The Natural* in the stadium when we were there that year. Robert Redford came into the locker room to meet all the coaches. He shook my hand and it's funny because he looked like he was seventy then from all the movie makeup and everything [Redford was in his late forties at the time]. Morgan Fairchild was dating the stage direction guy at that time, so she was always hanging around the stadium even though she wasn't in the movie. For a fourteen-year-old boy, it was great!"

Another unusual summer—by Matt Aker's standards—occurred in 1987 when the Cleveland Indians replaced their manager and most of the coaching staff, which included Jack.

"That was the first time we had a family summer. Once Dad got fired, he was being paid through the summer. We went and visited my brother and sister, who I did not know very well because they were from dad's first marriage. My brother lived in a little town called Menominee, Michigan, right on the Michigan-Wisconsin border. He ran a restaurant there. He's a professional chef who now runs a restaurant in Wisconsin. So, that summer we actually went and did things that we never really had time to do."

Matt Aker's son, Cole, was a pitcher in the St. Louis Cardinals organization, which drafted him in the fifteenth round in 2018 after he pitched at the University of North Carolina and University of Tampa. Another son, Blaine, chose not to pursue a baseball path. And Matt is a grandfather, courtesy of his daughter, who lives in Savannah, Georgia.

The wisdom Matt shared with his children was that which his father shared with him.

"One was to be a good person, as far as being somebody people could count on. But, really, the best [piece of advice] was with my career in baseball. He said, 'Don't ever walk away feeling like you didn't leave everything on the field.' Metaphorically, that transferred into life for me: Don't leave it 'on the field'; whatever you do, do your best."

Boog Powell and John W. Powell Jr.

Stealing (and Abandoning) the Groundskeepers' Cart

To a young generation of baseball fans, learning that the founder of Boog's Bar-B-Que at Camden Yards in Baltimore actually compiled a stellar career as a player is akin to music fans of a certain age learning that Paul McCartney was in another band before Wings. Such is the price of carving out a wildly successful second act in public life.

In Act One, John "Boog" Powell was one of the American League's most feared sluggers of the 1960s and 1970s. The 6-4, 230-pound first baseman joined the Baltimore Orioles in 1961 and when he was traded to the Cleveland Indians before the 1975 season, he left town as the Orioles' all-time home run leader with 303 (he now ranks third behind Cal Ripken Jr. and Eddie Murray).

Powell was the 1970 American League Most Valuable Player, after finishing runner-up to Harmon Killebrew the year before. Powell's 1970 numbers: thirty-five home runs, 114 runs batted in, 104 walks, a .297 batting average, and an OPS of .962. The Orioles won the World Series that fall, with Powell batting .294 with two home runs in the five-game series against Cincinnati.

Powell was a four-time all-star. He led the American League in slugging percentage in 1964, was the 1966 AL Comeback Player of the Year, and hit 339 home runs with 1,187 runs batted in over his seventeen-year career. He helped lead the Orioles to four World

Series appearances and was inducted into the team's Hall of Fame in 1979.

Act Two of Boog Powell's public life centered on the opening of Boog's Bar-B-Que at Camden Yards in 1992, coinciding with the opening of the ballpark. Located on the Eutaw Street promenade, the site is renowned among fans for its overstuffed Baltimore pit beef sandwiches, barbecue turkey, and pork.

Some might argue that Boog's Bar-B-Que is actually Powell's third act, the second one being a series of ten humorous Miller Lite television commercials he filmed in the 1970s and 1980s, often with former major league umpire Jim Honochick. In one, Honochick and Powell are debating the merits of Miller Lite. At the end of the conversation, Honochick puts on his glasses and exclaims with a trace of astonishment, "Hey, you're Boog Powell!"

Or, maybe it's actually Boog Powell's fourth act, since he also bought a marina in Key West, Florida, and managed a successful boat business there.

And about that nickname: Powell grew up in the south (Florida), where mischievous kids were sometimes called "buggers." Powell was called "Booger" and that eventually was shortened to "Boog."

◆

John Wesley Powell Jr. was born in Baltimore in 1963, his dad's third season with the Orioles. John Jr. was the only son of John and Janet "Jan" Powell, who also had two daughters, one of whom passed away in 2015. John Jr. has two children of his own, a son born in 2000 and a daughter born two years later. His earliest memories are dominated by baseball.

"It was a tremendous odyssey. Until I started getting old enough to go to the ballpark, it was pretty much either listening to the games on radio or watching on TV; mostly listening because back then there was very little TV coverage of the games. I can remember lying on the floor and listening to the old tube set radio late at night when they were playing on the West Coast. My grandfather used to take me to the ballpark to go see the games. We would always go to the games together and then go down to the clubhouse after the games. I don't know how it is nowadays, but back then once the game was over, we would all be able to go into the clubhouse and sit by Dad's locker and wait for him to get out of the shower or get through eating dinner or whatever he was doing. It was a great experience."

When the Orioles were on the road, many of the players' wives and kids hung out together.

"We used to hook up with them for, they call them play dates nowadays, but we used to just hang out and go into Baltimore or to Fort McHenry . . . different places just to let the kids burn off some steam. It was really cool. Brooks [Robinson] and his wife had three boys at that time. Dave McNally's oldest son was one of my best friends. Frank Robinson's son was a good friend of mine. At that time, we didn't have [mobile] phones and computers, so everybody was involved in the family unit thing. And, like I said, I don't know what it's like today, but back then the wives, the players, the kids all seemed to be a kind of cohesive unit.

"I used to pal around with Frank Robinson's kid in Baltimore. And then when Frank became the player-manager in Cleveland in '75, my dad got traded to Cleveland. We did some crazy things, Frank's son Kevin and I. The old stadium in Cleveland was a freakin' cavern. It was so big. And we used to steal the groundskeepers' cart and go driving it to the upper deck. And we'd be tooling around and the battery would go dead, and we'd just have to leave it wherever it was. I mean, sometimes it would be way, way out on the upper deck, overlooking Lake Erie. And we just walked back and we'd hear about it a day or two later" [laughs].

It would not be unusual to see players from the Orioles or other teams hanging out at the Powells' house in Baltimore.

"I remember several of the players, mostly the ones that had kids that were my age, coming over for barbecues. McNally was a good buddy. Brooks. Pat Dobson was probably one of his closest buddies. Curt Blefary. Andy Etchebarren. But [Dad] was also good friends with [opposing payers] Catfish Hunter and Sparky Lyle and whenever they came to town, if they had a Sunday game [often doubleheaders in those days, followed by a Monday off-day], they would come over after the game. I can remember many nights waking up at twelve or one o'clock in the morning and seeing the fire being lit. Ralph Salvon was the [Orioles] trainer, and we used to go to Ralph's house all the time for barbecues, and then he'd come over to our house now and then for barbecues."

The Powells lived in Baltimore year-round until John Jr. was two or three years old, and then built a house in Miami, which became their primary residence from that point forward.

"My dad wanted to be closer to home, and spring training was there, so it just made sense to be in Miami. Until I was around eight years old, we commuted back and forth. But it just got too difficult for my mom to take us out of school in Florida and then move us to school in Maryland [in the spring], and then take us out of school in Maryland in the fall and move us back to Florida. So, at that point, we stayed in Florida from September until school got out in May, and then we came back to Maryland."

The Powells' Miami house was approximately two thousand square feet on three-quarters of an acre, with an avocado grove on one side and a mango grove on the other. It was about three-quarters of a mile from John Jr.'s elementary school.

"We had a lot of really great neighbors, and being Boog's son really wasn't a big deal to any of them. I was just another kid in the neighborhood."

Sometimes, John Jr.'s day would start well before the first school bell rang.

"It would not be uncommon for me to be in bed at 4:30 or 5 o'clock in the morning and for [Dad] to come in and wake me up. He would make me breakfast and then we would go fishing from the shore. So, we would go fishing until 6:30, 7, 8:00, and then he would drop me off at school. On days when the weather was really good, he would get me up and we would just jump in the boat, sometimes with my mom and sisters. It wasn't uncommon for him to take us out of school because that window was so short. And it was really kind of cool because, with our extended family, there was always someone coming through, either one of my dad's aunts, uncles, or his dad or one of his brothers. And we would always be digging out a pit and cooking a pig or cooking ribs, cooking chickens. So, wintertime, off-season, was a great time around our house."

And it wasn't just family that stopped by.

"[Dad] was good friends with a lot of the Miami Dolphins players—Larry Csonka, Mercury Morris, Bob Griese. And then some of the guys from Baltimore they had—Earl Morrall, Don Shula. They were pretty tight. One of them gave me my first set of pads and helmet. They were all great guys."

Another perk that came with being a player's son was the thrill of air travel.

"From about the time I was, I want to say eight or nine, I used to go on at least one trip every summer. And it was cool because the team would have a charter flight or dedicated flight. And, back then, all the guys were smoking in the cabin, and they would drink and carry on, and they would always put me in the jump seat up with the pilot and copilot. And that was just great. And then when we'd get to Detroit or Cleveland or wherever the team was going, I was in the room with my dad and then I was at the ballpark with him."

In Baltimore, John Jr. would go with his dad to the ballpark pretty much every day during the summer.

"If I wasn't in school and the team was in town, when I was I wanna say eleven, twelve, thirteen, fourteen, I used to go to the ballpark every single day."

What did his dad and John Jr. talk about on their rides home after the games?

"He asked me if I met any nice girls. That was pretty much it."

John Jr. played baseball when he was young, a left-handed hitter and right-handed thrower like his dad. But father and son didn't have a whole lot of opportunity to play ball together.

"It was tough because he was always playing. And then when he was home in the winter, he had a hitting machine set up in the back-yard, but I couldn't do anything with that because of the level that he was doing. I was young, but I used to throw with him and get his arm loose. When I was anywhere from six to twelve, fourteen years old, I used to help him warm up."

John Jr. wasn't a natural at baseball.

"I played Little League in Baltimore. I was horrible. I struck out almost every time and everybody thought that I was a miserable fail-ure. In Miami, I started pitching. I had a good arm and I started hit-ting [better] as I got older. I played all the way through high school [in Key West, where the Powell family moved in 1974], but I wound up walking on as a tight end, defensive end, defensive and offensive tackle at the University of Florida. If I had to do it all over again, I probably would have stuck with baseball because I had a good arm. But baseball is a hard life. You have to really, really want to do it. I had enough times in my younger days when I didn't get to see my dad as much as I wanted to. So, I didn't think that was very appealing to me at that point in my life. Looking back on it, I might've pursued it a little bit harder, but I didn't do that.

"When I was in high school, [Dad] would give me some batting tips but, you know, I was a typical seventies kid. I just wanted to do it on my own. And he kind of let me be. He just said, 'If you want it, I'm here.' And I let it go. He's really a laid-back guy. I mean, if you want to know, he'll tell you, but if you don't want to know, he's just kind of laid-back."

John. Jr., a communications major, gave up football while in col-lege to devote his time to working at the school's radio station and newspaper.

After college, he worked as a "Howard Stern-kind of morning DJ" for eight years or so. His first on-air moniker was John Madison. Later, he adopted a new stage name.

"My middle name is Wesley and I had [an on-air] partner. His name was Dave. I decided I was going to be Wesley Allen, and that he was going to be Doyle Wrench. So, it was either the *Wes and Doyle Party* or the *Allen-Wrench Party* [laughs]. That was our thing. We did that for, like, four years. It was a lot of fun. It was an adventure. But we were making less than $300 a week, which was really kind of a slap in the face."

John Jr. left the fame and fortune of the radio business when Boog's Bar-B-Que opened at Camden Yards in 1992. It was an immediate hit, exceeding all expectations.

"We were pleasantly surprised, but we had to respond on the fly. We went from doing about $2,000 [per game] in gross dollar volume to $8,000. Next thing you know, we're at $40,000. And then we got as high as like $60,000. Those first eight years, the Orioles sold out every single game. We went from running out of food in the first inning to being able to stay open the whole game. It was just a matter of scaling up our operations, which I had a lot of help with, but I also had to work my ass off. It was a lot of hard work, but it was a lot of fun."

Boog was a big presence at the Eutaw Street site in those early years.

"He was always there. He was at the front of the line signing autographs and taking pictures. When he got tired, he would come back and hang out by the grill with me and he would realize that, wow, it's really hot back here and everybody's sweating their ass off, maybe I should go back up front where it's a little more tame.

"When we first started, I can remember him saying that this is only going to last for so long because people that knew [him] from [his] playing days are going to die off and [he] will no longer be relevant, but that never materialized. And that's because he was there all the time. There are a lot of copycat operations around the major leagues that use players' names and likenesses to do foodservice operations. But they don't have the presence that Boog provided at Orioles Park."

In 2000, John Jr. opened a Boog's Bar-B-Que in Ocean City, Maryland.

"That was my mainstay until COVID came and we closed. We really didn't have any choice; it was just a matter of economics. Also, it was difficult because we moved back to Florida in 2014 and I was commuting, and it was just very difficult."

In 2020, the Orioles purchased the rights to Boog's Bar-B-Que at Camden Yards. John Jr. still runs an operation at Ed Smith Stadium in Sarasota during the six weeks the Orioles hold spring training there.

"Ed Smith is great because it's not only Baltimore fans that are older and remember [the old] days, but we also have the Minnesota Twins [nearby]. And the Pittsburgh Pirates, Toronto [Blue Jays], the Yankees, and Red Sox. Everybody comes by to say hi, and even if [Boog] isn't there they just want to say, 'Hey we just wanted to tell you that we love your dad, and we're glad you're here and we love your food.' It's a great experience. The Ed Smith thing, I've gotten the most gratitude out of that than I have since probably the nineties. It's cool. And the other thing, too, is that it's only eight thousand or ten thousand people per game. It's not forty thousand. So, the pace is a bit less frenetic, and you can take a moment to wash your hands and shake hands with people and spend a minute to talk to them."

Having fans approach for conversation or autographs wasn't always a fun thing for John Jr. during his dad's playing career.

"I wouldn't say it was fun. It was a little bit invasive. It wasn't so bad in Florida, but in Maryland, especially when I got a little bit older, when he was home his schedule was pretty demanding. Lots of days, you might see him at one or two o'clock in the afternoon for an hour or two, and then he's got to go to work, and then we're in bed by the time he got home. So, if there was an off-day and we got to go out and, say, eat crabs, which we all really enjoyed, there's ten, twenty, thirty, forty people that are tapping him on the shoulder, wanting an autograph. And if you've ever eaten Maryland-style crabs, your hands are dirty. So, you've got to wipe your hands off in order to sign an autograph. And he never turned one down. So, it was a constant distraction. And, yeah, it was a little disturbing because we got to spend so little time with him. In Florida, we had his attention 100 percent. But in Maryland, when that window was so, so short, it was tough. To me, that was a difficult aspect of the whole relationship with baseball."

John W. Powell gives his dad Boog some batting tips at the 1966 World Series. The advice helped: Dad batted .357 in Baltimore's four-game sweep of Los Angeles. *John W. Powell*

Later, though, after his dad retired, the two had some great times together.

"It was freaking hilarious. When I was in college, I would frequently go and meet up with him anywhere that was geographically close enough for me to get to. He was working for the Miller Brewing Company. He was so busy. He used to do anywhere from 200 to 250 dates a year, traveling all over the country for them. I went to barbecue cook-offs in Texas. I did all the spring breaks on the East Coast. And, of course, I was in college, so I had the time of my life, but he was having a good time, too. Everybody knew him and it was a lot of fun. It was a lot more fun than the baseball days, I'll say that."

While in high school, John Jr.'s self-described "side hustle" was working at his dad's marina business in Key West.

"I worked at that all through high school. That was my first job, pumping gas, cleaning fish, cleaning people's boats, detailing boats."

Today, John Jr. does a bit of consulting work in the restaurant industry and is hoping to continue to operate the Ed Smith Boog's Bar-B-Que location. His sister is a mortgage loan officer, and, at her suggestion, he is working on getting his mortgage loan license.

He looks back on his childhood with extreme fondness.

"I was fortunate enough, along with my sisters, to be able to go to Key West High School and grow up on an island in the Caribbean [the Florida Keys are considered part of the American Caribbean]. It was just amazing. [Dad] had the marina and he really hadn't started traveling to do his Miller Lite work until after I graduated high school. It was an incredible experience for me to be able to grow up on the water. Honestly, unless I was playing baseball or basketball, I was either in the boat or in the water swimming. I keep telling my kids, we didn't have a computer. In Key West, we had two television channels and one PBS channel. And so, there was nothing else to do. We listened to music, and we went out on the boat and jumped in the water and swam all the time. Listening to my dad's stories about when he came to Key West, going out on the boat and seeing some of the things that he saw and some of the things that he did, I mean, I couldn't relate to the baseball stuff, but I could relate to what he saw in the water. And we were able to experience that together. And we still do."

Gil Hodges and Gil Hodges Jr.

Embracing the Legacy

Gil Hodges was a Hoosier, born in Princeton, Indiana, but he was revered in his adopted home in the New York City borough of Brooklyn. For proof of his standing among the hard-boiled Brooklyn citizenry, one need look no further than Google Maps. There, you will find the Marine Parkway–Gil Hodges Memorial Bridge, a span connecting Marine Park in Brooklyn with Rockaway in Queens. You'll see PS 193, The Gil Hodges School, at 2515 Avenue L. Over on Shell Road is Gil Hodges Field, a pair of Little League baseball diamonds whose basepaths, pitching mounds, and outfield grass have been trodden upon by tens of thousands of young ballplayers, many with major league dreams of their own. On Carroll Street is Gil Hodges Community Garden, a retreat for families and community groups. And you'll find Gil Hodges Way on Bedford Avenue, between Avenues L & N.

Hodges made his major league debut with the Brooklyn Dodgers in 1943, when he was nineteen years old. Shortly thereafter, he entered the Marine Corps and served as a gunner in the Sixteenth Anti-Aircraft Battalion. In 1945, now a Sergeant, Hodges participated in the Allied landing at Okinawa, earning him the Bronze Star for valor in combat.

After the war, Hodges resumed his playing career, making it back to the major leagues in 1947 as a backup catcher. There was little future at that position for Hodges, though, with future Hall of Fame catcher Roy Campanella on his way to Ebbets Field to stake his claim to the job. So Hodges was given a first baseman's glove, and he took to the position like a Brooklynite to pizza.

He was considered the finest defensive first baseman of his era, winning Gold Gloves for fielding excellence each of the first three years they were given out, from 1957 to 1959. Offensively, he was, in today's vernacular, a beast. The 6-1, 200-pound right-handed slugger led all major league first basemen of the 1950s in home runs, runs batted in, hits, runs scored, total bases, extra-base hits, and games played. He made the All-Star team eight times, from 1949 to 1955 and again in 1957. During his eighteen-year playing career in the major leagues (sixteen with the Dodgers and his final two with the New York Mets), Hodges hit 371 home runs with 1,274 runs batted in and an OPS of .846.

But Hodges is revered in Brooklyn for more than just stats. He was seen as a reliable, stand-up guy who was part of the community. Hodges was a man of quiet strength, but he would occasionally flex his muscles on the field, as when he helped protect Jackie Robinson in such a way that other teams, as well as his teammates, knew he always had the integration pioneer's back.

Hodges retired as a player early in the 1963 season, at the age of thirty-nine, to take over the managerial job of the Washington Senators. In 1968, the Mets brought favorite son Hodges back to New York to manage the six-year-old expansion franchise, one that had never come within sniffing distance of a winning record. The team went 73–89 during Hodges's first season at the helm, placing them ninth in the ten-team National League but representing their highest win total ever.

And then 1969 happened. The Mets combined stellar pitching and almost unfathomably timely hitting to win one hundred games during the regular season. They then vanquished the Atlanta Braves in three straight National League Championship Series games to advance to the World Series. There, they faced the heavily favored Baltimore Orioles and, after losing the series opener, went on to win four straight games and the World Series title. They were forever immortalized as the Miracle Mets.

Late in the 1968 season, Hodges suffered what was described at the time as a "mild heart attack." He returned to manage the Mets by spring training of 1969. On April 2, 1972, he played twenty-seven holes of golf with three of his Mets coaches at Palm Beach Lakes golf course in Florida. As the quartet walked back to their hotel, Hodges collapsed and died, the victim of a massive heart attack. He was forty-seven years old.

Hodges was voted into the Hall of Fame in Cooperstown in December 2021, an honor that many both in and out of baseball felt was long overdue.

◆

Gil Hodges Jr. was born March 12, 1950, the first of four children to Gil Sr. and Joan Hodges. Three girls were to follow.

"We grew up on East 32nd Street, between [Avenues] K and L. We had three bedrooms. The two older girls shared a room. The youngest, Barbara, hadn't been born yet. So, when she was born, we moved to Bedford Avenue, which was a bigger house and afforded us to all have our own bedrooms. I think that was 1962 or '63, just after Dad started playing for the Mets."

It took a while for Gil Jr. to recognize that his dad wasn't a typical nine-to-five guy like the other neighborhood fathers.

"I don't think that on East 32nd Street that perception of what my dad did for a living ever really took over. I remember Pee Wee [Reese] and Duke [Snider] coming to my house, sitting down; they were just people that my dad worked with. So, it really didn't take hold until later on. We moved out to California with the Dodgers in '58, and I remember '59 especially, when the Dodgers won the World Series. It was unbelievable, a terrific time. So, during that era, I was eight or nine, you start to put things together and realize this isn't a nine-to-five job."

When Gil Sr. was still playing, before he became a manager in the early 1960s, there was time for some father-son baseball instruction.

"We had a lot of time when he was a player. We would go to Marine Park in Brooklyn, a big baseball complex. And he would pitch to me. Mom and my sister would be in the outfield. Sometimes I would say to him, 'Come on, I want to see you hit the ball.'

"'That's not going to happen,' he'd say."

"Come on, please, just once."

Gil Sr. finally relented.

"The first pitch I threw him, he couldn't get to. The second pitch I threw him I'll never forget because as soon as I released the ball from my [right] hand, I felt a stinging in my left hand. He hit a line drive right into the glove. And he said to me, 'That's why I don't want to hit.' I'll never forget it. I mean, I could feel the sting and I never saw the ball!"

But, wait. Gil Hodges, *the* Gil Hodges, the all-star first baseman for the Brooklyn Dodgers, was playing ball with his family in Marine Park? That must have attracted quite a crowd of onlookers and autograph seekers.

"No, not at all. There were maybe twelve, fourteen different ball fields, and to see a father, a son and two females in the outfield would cause no distraction. No one would be close enough to walk by. We used to get that a lot later on in life when we went to the driving range. It's a lot closer and there's more contact when you walk by people, and people would stop and watch him hit a golf ball."

Back at home, his dad was the disciplinarian of the household.

"Mom's Italian. The great thing about Mom is the ability to, still to this day, yell, scream, vent, and thirty seconds later . . . totally gone, and we're back to where we were before. Dad was the disciplinarian. He had one steadfast rule, and it was pretty simple: Just don't lie. And there were times as a child that I lied to him. I mean, there were two times that I actually saw tears come down from his eyes. 'Cause he knew that I had lied to him. Those are things that stick with you and stay with you."

Discipline from his dad "was never a physical thing."

"I can't even tell you how strong he was. Rube Walker, who was Dad's pitching coach, and Joe Pignatano, who was his bench coach, were with him in Washington and later the Mets. He knew them from the Dodgers organization. They used to tell me stories about how guys would get to first base in the early '50s and start yelling at Jackie [Robinson], and Jackie would never yell back, and they would yell more and yell more and then maybe take one or two steps as if they were walking toward Jackie. And then all of a sudden, they felt the back of their uniform tugging them and taking them off the ground and putting them back on first base, which ended all the talk because they realized someone just picked them up and turned them around with one hand."

Gil Hodges was a leader off the field as well.

"When he was with the Dodgers, a bunch of players, maybe four or five of them, went to the race track, which you really weren't supposed to do. And the following day at a team meeting, [manager] Walter Alston said, 'I know some of you guys were at the track. I'd like you to leave $50 on my desk as a fine.'

"So, the meeting's over. The money is on Mr. Alston's desk. Dad walks in with $50. And Mr. Alston says, 'Gil, what are you doing?'"

"I'm leaving the $50 for being at the track."

"Gil, today's your lucky day."

"Why?"

"I didn't see you at the track."

"Dad said, 'That's okay, the other players did.' So, he put the $50 down and left."

As he entered his teens, Gil Jr. began to become more immersed in the baseball lifestyle.

"Being the only boy afforded me a lot of different things . . . my sisters [missed out on]. As I got older, especially in the summers when school was done, when Dad had the [managerial] job with the Senators, as soon as school would end, we would pack up the house on Bedford Avenue and move to Washington, D.C. We lived in the Shoreham Hotel, in a big suite. We all had our own rooms. I started to travel with the team in the summer, which was just, I mean, a child's dream. I could put on a uniform, take batting practice, take infield practice, and sit on the bench during the game, especially on road trips. I wouldn't do it at home because Dad felt I should sit in

Gil Hodges Jr. and his mom Joan chat with his dad before a game in 1963, when he was manager of the Washington Senators. *AP Images*

the stands with Mom and the girls. But on the road, it was just [us two], so he wanted to have me on the bench knowing where I was."

Junior quickly diffused any notion that he ever offered his dad "advice" during the game.

"Never. During the game, there was no interaction. I wouldn't even sit next to him. I'd sit down in the middle of the players and just try to watch and learn. I'd try to figure out what he was thinking. The interaction was more after the game when we would either go out to dinner or go back to the hotel. I would ask him questions and learn why he did what he did."

Later, Gil Jr. played first and third base for CW Post. Like his dad, Junior wore number 14, a literal target on his back for hecklers.

"You could feel like your life is under a microscope, or you could be so proud. Are you going to live your life saying that I have to carry this burden of being in the shadow of such a great athlete and even a greater man? One could embrace it and be thankful. And that's what I tried to do."

But he would hear the comments.

"A lot of the comments would be, especially on a close play at first base. If the umpire called them out, the other coach would run out and say, 'He took his foot off the bag, just like his father used to do.' I can remember little innuendos like that come out, but still, it was enjoyable.

"I used to play tripleheaders on Saturdays at the Parade Grounds, and on Sundays a doubleheader because they had to allow time to go to church in the morning. So, playing five games every weekend was just fun, just something that I enjoyed doing.

"My dad's philosophy, and we had this meeting just once, but I'll never forget it—and it was just, 'I really don't care what you want to do as you grow older. All I want to do is make sure that you do it to the best of your ability, regardless of what it is. If it's athletics, terrific. If it's science, terrific. If it's the medical field, terrific. It doesn't matter to me. I never want you to feel the pressure of having to follow in my footsteps.'"

But follow in his dad's footsteps he did. Gil Jr. was selected by the Mets in the twenty-seventh round of the 1971 amateur draft, following his junior year at CW Post. He signed a professional contract and played for Mets minor league teams in Marion, Virginia, and Pompano Beach, Florida.

"We had some arguments about [leaving college with a year to go], but I promised to go back later to get the degree. You know, you get so excited and you're always fearful that if you don't sign, the following year you could get hurt. You could have a bad year and lose the opportunity. Through probably my total annoyance to my dad and a lot of help from my mother, we were able to convince him that I should at least give it a shot.

"I went to Marion, rookie ball. And I did well. And then I got moved up the following year to the Florida State League, which was Class A ball. And that was just about the time that Dad passed. I was in a bad frame of mind and wanted to move away from the Mets organization. I got signed by the Cardinals to play on their double-A team, but I banged up my shoulder pretty well. I had to wrap it up."

He did, in fact, eventually go back to school to earn his college degree.

Gil Jr. got married in February 1972. In April, tragedy struck. It was Easter Sunday, two days before the former Dodger and now Mets manager was to turn forty-eight years old.

"I saw Dad on Saturday in St. Petersburg, where the Mets used to train. My wife and I, on Sunday, went to church late afternoon. I think it was a five o'clock mass. We came out of church and heard on the radio that Gilbert Hodges died. And my wife said, 'That's not your father.' I think there was a newscaster named Gilbert Hodges, so I instantly made that connection. And then the story reran about thirty seconds later, and it ended up being Dad. So, I heard it on the radio, which was kind of tough."

On the previous day, when Gil Jr. saw his dad in West Palm Beach, the two parted ways at the hotel elevator.

"He said, 'Watch over Mom.' Looking back, it was like he had a premonition."

At the funeral, Gil Jr. shared a moment with Jackie Robinson, a moment that spoke volumes about what Gil Sr. had meant to the man who broke baseball's color barrier a generation earlier.

"Dad and Jackie were very close. And Mom and Rachel (Jackie's wife) were very close. Mom was a big proponent of other wives befriending Rachel. She would bring Rachel to the house and the other wives would come, which made it somewhat easier not only for Rachel, but for Jackie, too. So, there was a tremendous amount of mutual respect. And when Dad passed, Howard Cosell was at the funeral. And he asked me to please come outside. He said, 'I need you to come with me.' So, we turned the corner and there was a car. And he said, 'I just need you to get into the back seat.'

"I opened the door and get into the back seat and there's Jackie, just hysterical. And he just hugs me and kisses me and says to me, 'Next to my son's passing, this is the worst day of my life.' And he couldn't talk anymore, just kept crying. And I said, 'It means so much to me because I know he loved you and you loved him.'"

Earlier, Gil Sr. had suffered a heart attack while managing a game for the Mets in September 1968. As he convalesced that winter, one wonders whether Joan or the kids mentioned the possibility of Gil Sr. stepping down from the stressful managerial job.

"Not if you value the daylight, that's the best way I could put it. He would never have thought about that. That subject is so far removed from any topic of conversation that if the thought even entered my mom's mind the best thing to do was squash it and throw it away and make sure it never came back. We knew better. And then, of course, we turned around and, boom, we win the World Series."

The 1969 Mets, with Gil Hodges at the helm and young Tom Seaver, a future Hall of Famer, on the mound, stunned the baseball world by winning the championship.

"The only thing that my father asked of them is that every time you get dressed and go on that field, it's 100 percent. Someone who grasped that very rapidly was number 41 [Seaver]. He just took that in and realized what it meant and helped spread that through the players because he didn't want to lose anymore. He didn't want to be a .500 ballclub. You're not a winner, you're mediocre. And he thought they were all better than mediocre. Tom always said that next to his dad, there was nobody closer [to him] than my father."

The pair only had two more seasons together before Gil Sr.'s fatal heart attack in 1972. Years later, a similar ailment nearly befell young Gil.

"In 2015, I came down to Florida to have Thanksgiving with my sister. And I actually had a heart attack, on Thanksgiving Day. And I went to the emergency room. And it's funny because if I was in Brooklyn, I would never have gone to the emergency room on Thanksgiving Day because, in my mind, it's a three-hour wait. In Palm Beach Gardens? It's, 'You're having heart pain, get on a gurney.' So, I ended up getting a stent.

"The doctor comes in the following morning, and he asks if there are any hereditary heart ailments in your family. I said, Dad's side. Dad passed away at forty-seven, his brother at forty-eight, and their father at fifty, all from heart disease. So, they started to do more research on what I had and found out that it takes twenty or twenty-five years to develop, which I'm pretty sure that's what happened to my dad. Except it didn't happen late enough for science to catch up to it.

"I am so proud of what he was able to accomplish, even in his short lifetime, and the way people still talk to me about him; like they had dinner with him last month! So, those are the things that I hang on to that make me proud of who he was, and the legacy that he left behind. I mean, to have little leagues and bridges and schools named after him, and to have the pastor at mass say, 'It's too hot for a sermon, please keep the ten commandments and say a prayer for Gil Hodges.'"

Gil Hodges Jr. has a son and two daughters. After his fling with minor league baseball, he came home to run Gil Hodges Lanes, a forty-eight-lane, family-owned bowling center in Brooklyn. After that business was sold, Hodges worked for fifteen years as an account executive for Merrill Lynch and E.F. Hutton. Most recently, he was chief operating officer at Frenchman's Creek Beach and Country Club in Palm Beach Gardens, Florida.

"I think Dad would be proud that his children—although the courses were not always straight and narrow and easy—developed into some relatively good people."

Author's Update: Joan Hodges, the matriarch of the Hodges family, died on September 17, 2022 at the age of 95.

Tony Peña and Tony Peña Jr.

Poking Sleeping Players with Toothpicks

Tony Peña's long major league career as a catcher can best be described in one word: *dependable.*

Peña played eighteen seasons in the major leagues with the Pittsburgh Pirates (1980–1986), St. Louis Cardinals (1987–1989), Boston Red Sox (1990–1993), Cleveland Indians (1994–1996), and a 1997 swan song with the Chicago White Sox and Houston Astros. During this period, Peña led the league five times in games caught and finished second three other times. Today, more than two decades after his retirement as a player, Peña still ranks seventh all-time in most games caught (1,950).

But Peña did much more than just show up. He excelled.

He was a five-time all-star who was awarded four Gold Glove Awards for fielding excellence. He twice led the National League in assists by a catcher and was a four-time league-leader (twice in each league) in catcher double-plays, usually of the "strike-'em-out, throw-'em-out" variety.

He was instantly recognizable for what was then a unique catching style in which he stuck his left leg straight out and kept his right knee on the ground with no runners on base so he could get down low and "steal" low strikes for his pitchers. Peña was pitch-framing years before most of us ever heard the term.

The Dominican Republic native was an outstanding hitter as well. He twice finished in the top ten in the National League in batting average, not an easy feat for catchers, who always lead the league in wear and tear, and bumps and bruises.

Peña played for two pennant-winning teams, the 1987 St. Louis Cardinals and the 1995 Cleveland Indians. In the 1987 World Series, he batted .409 with a .935 OPS, and over his entire postseason career batted a robust .338/.834 over seventy-eight plate appearances.

Unfortunately, his teams lost both World Series in which he played. He did, however, get his elusive World Series Championship ring as bench coach for the New York Yankees in 2009. He was a coach for New York from 2006 to 2015.

Earlier, he managed the Kansas City Royals from 2002 to 2005 and was named American League Manager of the Year in 2003. In 2013, he managed the Dominican Republic team to the championship of the World Baseball Classic with a perfect 8–0 record, the first team to ever go undefeated in the tournament.

Peña was inducted into the Caribbean Baseball Hall of Fame in 2016.

◆

Tony Peña Jr. was born on March 23, 1981, in the Dominican Republic province of Santiago, just as his father was winding down spring training in Florida with the Pirates. Tony Jr. was the first-born child of Tony Sr. and Amaris Peña, who later had two more children, one girl and one boy. The family's home base was in Santiago, but they spent many months each year in the United States.

"During the summers, once school season would end, I would come to the states and spend time with my dad, whatever city he would be in.

"In Boston, during the game, we would make a baseball out of a sanitary sock, and we would put tape around it. During the game, we would be playing inside the clubhouse. They had a three-foot-wide hallway, and we would play from one end to the other end. We had a little scoring system and all that.

"When my dad was with the Pirates, I remember parts of it. Cecilio Guante, Jose DeLeon, Rafael Belliard, and Ruben Rodriguez, since my dad was in the big leagues already, they would get called up and he would have them stay at his house so they didn't have to spend money on rent or anything like that. Raffi [Belliard] always tells me, 'You used to get a little toothpick and poke us in the feet,' and I'd be like, 'Come on, let's go play.' I was like five, six years old at the time.

"The time I kinda remember [best] as a kid was when he was with the Indians because I was thirteen, fourteen years old. So, I had an idea of what was going on in my surroundings, you know what I mean? The friends that you had growing up most of the time were other players' kids, 'cause you're around them the entire day at the field or during the game in the family rooms.

"I would go with my dad to the field. Sometimes, I would go up early with him [for] practice and it was a very nice opportunity. You grew up around all the big leaguers. Like Manny Ramirez was there, and you look back in time and you're like, 'Wow, I was around guys like Manny and Eddie Murray, who is a Hall of Famer.' My dad's locker was in the middle of Manny and Eddie Murray. How cool was that?

"I remember, it was crazy because Michael Jordan started playing baseball and was in spring training [with the Chicago White Sox] when Dad was with the Indians. So, people would ask [me], 'Can you get Michael to sign this?' And I would be going over and over, and he would sign. I just kept going back to Jordan to get autographs, and he just kept signing them. And now I look back, like, wow, that's why he was one of the best, just by how he handled it.

"Life as a kid was always baseball, baseball, baseball. But for me to be able to play baseball, I had to get good grades. So [Dad] was always on top of me, pushing me to, 'Hey, if you don't [get good grades], I'm not gonna let you go and play.' So that was a fear factor. If I didn't do good, I wasn't going to be able to play baseball. That was his way of pushing us to do things the right way."

Playing Little League baseball in Boston is a particularly fond memory for Tony Jr.

"It was a pretty cool experience with my dad being able to go to some of the games. And the kids would come around and he'd sign autographs and that would always make you feel good; feel special."

Baseball always came naturally to Tony Jr.

"It's the only thing I saw growing up. Seeing my dad and the way he would work and just dedicate his life to the game. I mean, the season would end in major league baseball, and he would take a week off and the next week he would be playing winter ball. It just shows the love he had for the game, and the appreciation. He would play non-stop. You look back like, wow, how did he do that?"

Winter ball was a special time for Tony Jr.

"In winter ball I would be able to be in the dugout. I would be the batboy, I'd be a ball boy. So, I was there next to him. It was a dream. I remember on weekends after winter ball games, they would stay in the clubhouse just talking baseball. Whenever it was the weekend, I would be able to stay. During the week, they would send me home [so I could] get some sleep and be ready for school the next day."

But while Tony Jr. inherited his dad's love of the game, he did not follow in his footsteps in donning the "tools of ignorance" worn by catchers.

"Growing up, seeing Ozzie Smith with the Cardinals, I remember him making diving plays and jumping in the air and I was like, wow, that's cool! And then, in Cleveland, Omar Vizquel was there. So, it was just my favorite position after seeing those two guys play shortstop the way they played it. Plus, I wasn't big [enough] to be a catcher [laughs]."

Was his dad disappointed?

"I don't know if he wanted me to be a catcher or not, but my brother [Francisco, who played in the major leagues from 2014 to 2018], he's a catcher. And when my brother was little, he would throw with his left hand and my dad actually switched him to where he would throw with his right hand because he wanted him to be a catcher. He was a little bit stockier. So, my brother eats left-handed, writes left-handed, but throws right-handed."

Tony Jr. was signed by the Atlanta Braves as an amateur free agent in 1999.

"[Dad] didn't want to push us in any way. When he started to work with us more and just talk to us was once we were playing professional baseball. He would give us advice on how to go through the tough times. In baseball, there are a lot of ups and downs. You gotta be strong mentally to be able to push through this game.

Tony Peña Jr. (right) with his dad and brother Francisco in Cleveland. *Tony Peña Jr.*

"I don't think there was added pressure [being the son of a major league player], but you could feel that people expected you to be better or the same as your dad."

Tony Jr. got called up to the big leagues by the Braves in April 2006.

"I got called up because I think Chipper [Jones, the Braves' third baseman] had gotten hurt. I called my dad and mom right away. They were just so happy because, you know, in this game you put in a lot of work and a lot of sacrifice, and they know what it takes to be up there. And not many people get the opportunity to be a father-son combination in the big leagues. The number one thing [Dad] told me was just 'proud of you,' and that this was just the beginning because it takes a lot of work to stay up there. 'Just go up there, have fun, behave, and you know the things you have to do.'"

Tony Jr. found it advantageous to have grown up around big league ballparks and players.

"It definitely helped out because you already had an idea of how to handle yourself. You know, a lot of things can be thrown at you, and you have no idea how to react. But, for me, it was something that fortunately I already had a little bit of experience, being around my dad and seeing how he handled all that.

"I ended up being up there like three or four months of the season. Chipper got hurt, then [Edgar] Renteria [a shortstop] got hurt. Then, the next year, I got traded to Kansas City."

Tony Jr. played with the Royals from 2007 to 2009 but broke his hamate bone, a small bone in the wrist, in his final season.

"When I came back, I didn't have any confidence hitting. So, I ended up pitching for the Royals [in the minor leagues] the last month and a half, two months of the season. The next year I ended up signing with the [San Francisco] Giants. I made it all the way up to Triple-A with them and the next year I signed with the [Boston] Red Sox. I ended up being pitcher of the year in Triple-A with them but never got called up. I ended up playing like ten years as a pitcher between the minor leagues and Mexico."

Tony Jr.'s position change to pitcher resulted in some memorable moments in winter ball. He was teammates with his brother, the catcher, on Aguilas and got to pitch to him.

"Sometimes I would shake him off and shake him off and he would just go, 'Throw whatever you want.'"

When asked which he enjoyed more, playing shortstop or pitching, Tony Jr. smiles and says, "Playing baseball!"

Late in his career, those early years of juggling schoolwork with being at the ballpark paid off.

"That actually helped me along the way. Growing up, I was always in a baseball stadium, but I always found a way to do homework. So, later on in my career, around 2013, I decided to go to college online. I already had experience on how to juggle my time, so I ended up graduating from the University of Phoenix."

His playing career ended in 2017 when he was released by his team in Mexico.

"I was like, okay, I was thirty-six and I played enough. This is good enough. So, I ended up retiring and that same year I called the Royals to let them know I was gonna retire and if they had anything they needed, I'm interested in coaching and was up to learn. And I actually got a phone call a couple of weeks later. They needed someone to fill in. And that's how my career in coaching got started."

Peña eventually served on the Royals' major league staff and in 2022 managed one of their minor league affilliates.

Any aspiration to manage in the big leagues, like his dad?

"That's something I don't think about too much. If it happens, it happens. As long as I'm working in baseball and enjoying being around the guys trying to help them fulfill their dreams, that's all that matters. That's what you're here for when you're a coach. You're just trying to help someone else fulfill their dream and, hopefully, they can do what they want to do."

14

Jim Bouton and Michael Bouton

Riding Upside Down to Yankee Stadium

In an age when the New York Yankees and their buttoned-down, methodical churning out of pennants were compared to the then corporate behemoth U.S. Steel, pitcher Jim Bouton stood out as an iconoclast who didn't quite fit the mold; ironic in a way, because Bouton loved playing the game as much as anyone.

Bouton was signed by the Yankees as a nineteen-year-old in 1958. The right-hander pitched well in the minor leagues and made the major league roster out of spring training in 1962. His first major league start, on May 6, 1962, versus the Washington Senators, was emblematic of the way starting pitchers were used at the time: He allowed seven hits and walked seven batters but was allowed to throw a complete game shutout. Needless to say, pitch counts were not yet a thing.

The following season is when Bouton emerged as a star. He won twenty-one games despite not joining the starting rotation until May 12. He pitched in that summer's All-Star Game and started game three of the World Series against the Los Angeles Dodgers, throwing seven innings of one-run ball but losing, 1–0, to Don Drysdale.

Nineteen-sixty-four was another big year for "Bulldog" Bouton, as he won eighteen games, led the American League with thirty-seven games started, and pitched brilliantly in the World Series. Bouton was 2–0 in the Fall Classic, allowing just three runs in 17.1 innings. The Yankees lost that series in seven games. Unbeknownst to all, the 1964 World Series would mark the end of the Yankees dynasty that dated back to the Babe Ruth–Lou Gehrig years, and it would also mark the end of Jim Bouton's excellence as a major league pitcher. Only twenty-five years old that fall, Bouton, plagued by arm trouble, would never again win more than four games in any season.

In 1968, the Yankees sold Bouton's contract to the Seattle Pilots, an expansion team that was to begin play during the 1969 season. In August 1969, Bouton was traded to the Houston Astros, and he pitched for them until being released in the summer of 1970. But he loved playing the game and continued to compete in the minor leagues, the Mexican League, independent league baseball, and adult leagues, before resurfacing in the major leagues in 1978 as a knuckleball pitcher for the Atlanta Braves. On September 14, 1978, Bouton beat the San Francisco Giants, 4–1, for his final major league victory. He retired for good after that season.

Off the field, Bouton marched to his own drummer. As a rookie with the Yankees, he enjoyed playing practical jokes and entertaining his teammates with his impression of Crazy Guggenheim, a character played by Frank Fontaine on *The Jackie Gleason Show*. What Yankee management found decidedly less funny was Bouton's penchant for haggling over his contract every year. In those pre–free agency days, players were bound to their teams until they were traded, sold, or released, and were offered one-year contracts every winter, often for insultingly paltry sums. Bouton also was outspoken on political issues, such as apartheid in South Africa, a rarity for his day and a trait that also rubbed management, as well as some teammates and fans, the wrong way.

During his partial season with the Pilots, Bouton took notes and spoke into a tape recorder for a book that was to change the face of sports journalism and the way many fans viewed players. *Ball Four*, written in collaboration with sportswriter Leonard Schecter, was published in the spring of 1970. It gave readers an inside look into the lives of players off the field, from the clubhouse to the bedroom. To say it was controversial does not do justice to the firestorm it caused. Bouton was summoned to meet with baseball Commissioner Bowie Kuhn, who publicly condemned the book. Many ex-teammates were furious, with some promising physical retribution (none occurred). The Yankees essentially made Bouton persona non grata in their organization, leaving their former star pitcher off the invitation list for the team's annual Old Timers' Game, a congenial gathering of former players who are feted on the field and enjoy a day or two of laughs, a lot of reminiscing, and perhaps an adult beverage or two. This cold war lasted until 1998, and it took a Bouton family tragedy—the death of his daughter, Laurie, in an automobile accident in 1997—to serve as the catalyst for Bouton's triumphant return to Yankee Stadium thanks to an op-ed piece published in the *New York Times* by his son, Michael.

It should be noted that while vast attention was paid to the juicier portions of *Ball Four*, the book's central theme was Bouton's love for playing the game. The book's final line sums it up: "You see, you spend a good piece of your life gripping a baseball, and in the end it turns out it was the other way around all the time."

Bouton wrote other books, worked as a sportscaster, and spoke on college campuses. He died at the age of eighty in 2019 at his home in Great Barrington, Massachusetts. He suffered a stroke in 2012 and revealed in 2017 that he had a brain disease linked to dementia.

◆

Michael Bouton was born in Ridgewood, New Jersey, on October 26, 1963, at the zenith of his father's major league career and just twenty days following the end of that year's Yankees-Dodgers World Series. He was introduced to the itinerant baseball lifestyle at an early age.

"I went to kindergarten in Wyckoff, New Jersey, and Houston, Texas. First and second grade in Wyckoff, and fourth through tenth in the Englewood, New Jersey, school system (he skipped the third grade). I went to Teaneck High School [in New Jersey] in eleventh and twelfth grades. I went to school in Florida and Knoxville, Tennessee, for little bits of time."

Did he have a favorite place?

"I guess I never really thought of it like that. I mean, every place had something interesting. Like, we lived among extreme poverty in Durango, Mexico, and yet there was beauty. We had neighbors who would offer us fresh goat milk. Savannah, Georgia, I remember as a nice place with a beautiful ballpark, Grayson Stadium."

As a boy, Michael would often ride to Yankee Stadium with his dad and Uncle Bob.

"I would ride to the games, basically upside down, looking through the windshield at what passed above us. So, I knew where we were by what I could see above me. When we would get to the Third Avenue Bridge, I knew that we were almost there, and I would sit upright. I remember playing that game. And now I'm guessing that the game was an effort to shut me up [laughs]."

After the games, Michael would often join his dad in the Yankee clubhouse.

"I remember it was a dank kind of place. There was this huge ventilation system that opened up in such a way that, as a kid, I associated it with the calliopes that I saw outside the stadium. I remember Mickey Mantle. He had an aura, like when you see paintings of the saints with a glow. It wasn't just the lights reflecting off his blond hair. He had his own light; he glowed. I knew he was a special person in the room without even being told.

"So, we would go to the game and sit in the family section. My mom, I wouldn't say she was an outcast, but there was a hierarchy in place, and my mom was a newbie. And my mom didn't fit in with the mink-stole crowd 'cause that's just not her speed; that's not our style. So, my mom got along with some of the more eccentrics. She was friends with Diane Pepitone, who was very down to earth. I had a thing for Diane Pepitone from, like, as early as I can remember. I can remember wanting to be on her lap [laughs]."

As might be expected, it took young Michael a while to understand that his dad made a living in a rather unique way.

"I thought everybody's dad played for a team [laughs]. It was like, 'What team does your dad play for?' But hold on, when you think of it, I'm really not that far off because, you know, your dad works for IBM, well, that's his team. Your dad sells pizza? Well, then, that's his team. That's how it was to me. I didn't really understand."

Michael relates a story that his dad would tell on the speaking circuit.

"He starts off with a story of how I found out that he was a famous baseball player. He was getting off an airplane and he was walking

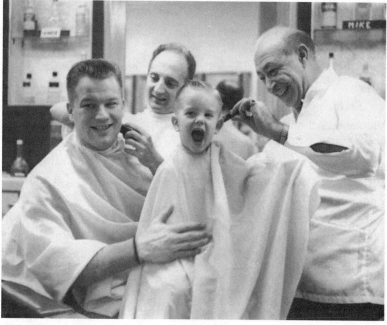

Michael Bouton gets his first haircut on the lap of his dad, Jim. *Michael Bouton*

through the little corridor thing. And he bends down to call me and I'm shy and standoffish and I don't run to him the way I normally do. And he asked me what's up. And, apparently, I bashfully said to him, 'Hey Dad, you're Jim Bouton, aren't you?' And that's his icebreaker. He'd get an opening laugh with that. I don't know how much of it is me remembering having read that story and how much of it is me remembering the actual event."

Michael's boyhood memories are particularly strong from the time his family moved to Seattle.

"There was a TV show that was popular when we moved out there, *Here Come the Brides* with Bobby Sherman, and the theme song, *Seattle*, had a lyric about 'the bluest skies you've ever seen.' And that's how we felt. You know, the enthusiasm, the bright-eyed enthusiasm of that song, I would say really followed our family during that period of time. We had a great time exploring the Northwest. We went to different Native American sites, and I think that, as someone who later became an environmentalist, I would say that trip had a great impact on me."

Seattle, of course, is where Jim Bouton wrote the legendary *Ball Four*.

"I remember when Dad was writing the book. I had a fight with the neighborhood bully, and I came up [into the house], and I was scared. And Dad's just typing away and he's telling me, 'Don't worry about him.' He says, 'Look, you're the underdog. You know what they never expect from the underdog? If he takes a swing at you, you punch him in the nose hard. Once.' I went out there, knocked that kid out. He never bothered me again. And, in a sense, Dad was kind of doing the same thing with his words when he was writing. He was throwing his punch at Major League Baseball's reserve clause and the lack of free agency."

Exploring the Northwest was just one of the many experiences that Jim and his wife, Bobbie, gave young Michael.

"Dad used to know how important it was to give us certain experiences. Some of those things he was criticized for, like the fact that he kept us in public schools, especially for a period of time in Englewood where it was a minority-majority school. A lot of our relatives and friends were critical of my father for doing that, but my father felt it was important to take a progressive stance. I think that, ultimately, it was a good decision that he made us mix with people of different backgrounds.

"He'd take us to carnivals. Sometimes, we would travel with the team when they would play in other small towns. And there would be state fairs we would go to, and we would taste the flavor of wherever it was. A lot of these fairs would have these sideshows where you would pitch and try to knock over rows of milk bottles. And Dad would take the challenge and we'd figure out that most of those milk bottle ones are scams. He would hit one of them with like an eighty-eight-mile-an-hour fastball [and nothing would happen]."

A Jim Bouton fastball was not something that Michael would see from his dad when the two played catch in the backyard.

"Basically, we were guinea pigs for Dad's knuckleball. He would warm up with us. He would never throw his fastest pitch. As I got older, like seventeen, I wanted to take cuts on him, and it pissed me off that he wouldn't do it. He was afraid that [a pitch] would get away from him."

In Englewood, Michael and his brother played Little League ball for the first time.

"David [his adopted brother] and I were kind of forced into it. I mean, we obviously knew the rules 'cause we'd been to enough games, and we threw the ball with Dad and would occasionally take cuts against him, even though he wasn't throwing us his best stuff. But we never played in a team situation. When we moved to Englewood, he threw us into the mix because he wanted us to participate in integrating the league. There were a lot of white families that would not place their kids on black teams. And so, my dad wanted to make sure that he did. He wanted to make a political statement and we were part of that. [Our coach's] philosophy was every kid plays; every kid gets in the game. And so, Dad decided that's the team we were going to be on. We were basically the Bad News Bears. We didn't win many games, but everybody played, and we had pizza afterwards. And one game I asked if I could pitch. I thought I could. And I discovered that the distance between the pitcher's mound and home plate was a lot further than I thought [laughs]. So, I had no ideas of following in my dad's footsteps or anything like that."

Instead, Michael took up ballet.

"My goal getting into ballet was to make it to Broadway. I wanted to be a dancer. I wanted to be Ben Vereen. I figured the best ticket to be Ben Vereen was going to be learning how to dance classically and getting all the basics down first. So, I decided to pursue ballet."

Michael's parents fully supported his ballet pursuit.

"Dad would go out of his way to talk to the press, to comment on the athleticism of the dancers. It was an interesting period. It was about seven years of my life. But ever since I was a kid I was interested in politics, and it was around that time that I decided to put my egotistical dreams of being a Broadway star on hold and focus on doing what I could to save the environment."

Perhaps surprisingly, Michael says his work as an environmental activist was not directly attributable to his father's own beliefs.

"My dad did something that was really uncool when I was a young kid, and it was only for 300 bucks or something like that. He did an ad for the timber industry sometime in the seventies when we were out in Portland, [Oregon]. There was a family discussion on whether he should take the $300 and do the ad or whether he should turn it down. We had a family vote, and I persuaded my mom and my sister [Laurie], and my dad had David, so it was 3–2 and my dad overruled us. I opposed Dad on that one, but truth be told, we were on the same side more often than not."

Portland is where Jim Bouton played for a brief time with the Mavericks, an independent team in the Northwest League. The team was immortalized in the 2014 documentary film, *The Battered Bastards of Baseball.*

"That's a fantastic story. One time [the team] was behind schedule on the bus trying to go to whatever game they were trying to get to. And the batboy, Todd Field, the [future] Academy Award–nominated director, had to go to the bathroom and they didn't want to stop the bus. So, they took him down the stairwell of the bus and my father and one of the other players grabbed him by the arms and they opened the doors, and he took a whiz while they were going down the highway at like a hundred miles an hour."

Life began to change for Michael when his parents divorced in 1981 following a separation that began in 1978.

"It came right after his first start with Atlanta. It happened that night. It's all fucked up. Dad asked Peter Golenbock [a writer and friend of Jim's] to chaperone Paula [later to become Jim's second wife] to Atlanta as a friend of his—like to pretend Paula was Pete's friend. He had never met Paula before, but he was playing it off as a favor for my dad. Peter says that to this day it's one of his biggest regrets. We knew as a family that my mom and dad were going to have a trial separation at the end of the year. We knew that [in] early summer. All of us kids, we were ready for that. We did not know there was another woman.

"Ultimately, Dave and I moved in with my father. But for the first year, we went back and forth between houses. My dad rented a small house in Englewood, and we would spend three days a week there and three days a week at my mom's and a half-day between each place. And that got to be a pain. I know he tried. In fact, he did a lot of really great things during that period of time. He did teach David and I how to make breakfast for ourselves and how to fry an egg correctly. My mom taught me a lot of cooking stuff. Thanks to my mom, I have a lot of great recipes that I can make now. But Dad taught me how to cook an egg."

Tragedy rocked the family in August 1997 when the Boutons' only daughter, Laurie, died in an automobile crash at the age of thirty-one. The devastating event prompted Michael to write an op-ed published by the *New York Times* the following Father's Day, a piece that urged the Yankees to reconsider what, in effect, was their blacklisting of Jim Bouton from participating in their annual Old Timers' Day celebrations, a fallout of *Ball Four*. That year's Old Timers' Day was scheduled for the following month.

"It was intended to be published as a New Year's resolution piece. That was my original goal. I realized after a while that I wasn't going to make the New Year's deadline. It didn't have that ring of truth, the ring of finality, that it was perfect. So, I missed New Year's. I missed my dad's birthday, March 8. So, Father's Day was basically my last shot to get it right. I finished it that Thursday night. I called Ira Berkow [a *Times* sportswriter], who was in Chicago. He gave me the fax number of his editor, Tom Jolly. I sent it in, and very shortly thereafter my phone is ringing and it's Tom Jolly and, yes, he's very interested and wants to know if I have a photo of Laurie. I had just moved, so I had stuff in boxes. I went through my stuff and found the photograph. The next day I went in with Melanie [Michael's fiancée at the time] and there were these guards waiting for me and they took me right past security, boom, boom. And the rest is history."

In the op-ed, Michael wrote:

"I am hoping to reach George's [Steinbrenner's] sons. Despite our different upbringings, I think we have a lot in common. It's never easy growing up the child of a public figure. I know they have heard mean things said about their father, much the same way I have. I think there have been days when they have been publicly embarrassed by him and there have been times when they have been as proud as any child has ever been about a parent—exactly like me.

I'm sure they love their father as much as I love mine. That's what Father's Day is about—celebrating that love.

"I see this as an opportunity to get my father some extra hugs at a time in his life when he could use all the hugs he can get. It is something he would never seek for himself—he is going to kill me when he reads this—and maybe the kind of thing only a son or daughter can do for their father."

In the op-ed, Michael also cited Yogi Berra's estrangement from the Yankees, writing: "I have applauded Yogi's decision on this matter of principle, but recently I had a change of heart and mind. It is just as petty for Yogi to spite George as it is for George to spite my father. It does not serve the greater good for families, the fans or the sport."

The article had its intended effect.

"I gave George a path to Yogi, and that is the only reason my letter worked. I was sure the call [from the Yankees] was going to come."

It did, and Jim Bouton took the field at Yankee Stadium, wearing his pinstriped uniform number 56, for the first time in some thirty years. The fans welcomed him with a loud and prolonged ovation.

"I guess maybe he was apprehensive that maybe someone would say something nasty to him, but I think he realized that the dynamics created a situation where nobody would dare say shit to him, that if they did it would reflect rather poorly on them. Maybe there was some apprehension whether the fans would cheer him or not because a number of years [earlier] he was booed at Shea Stadium right after the publication of Ball Four. So, Dad still had that in his head."

Before the on-field ceremonies, father and son were interviewed by ABC World News.

"My dad made a demand of me that for the interview I show up in a suit and tie, and I'm like, 'Dad, I don't want to wear a suit and tie.' He said, 'Please, do me a favor and show up in a suit and tie and don't show up dressed like a hippie.' I said, 'Dad, I'll be dressed fine. I'll come like I'm dressed to go to a ballgame. I'll be comfortable. I'll look fine.' He said no, it's gotta be a suit and tie. So, I show up to the interview, I'm in a suit and tie, and guess who's dressed casually for a fucking ballgame? I think he was just thinking of what would reflect best on him, and that was the first thought that crossed his mind. It was a little bit of Dad's ego and self-centeredness that would reflect back on him from time to time."

The interview kerfuffle notwithstanding, Michael's op-ed turned out to be one of the great Father's Day gifts of all time.

"It was the gift that kept on giving. It was something that every year we would revisit. But, to be fair, I think he knew on some level that I didn't just write it for him. It was really written for Laurie. Dad didn't give a shit whether he ever went back to Yankee Stadium or not. And that's the truth of it. That was something Laurie wanted. And that's why I did it. I was delivering Laurie's last gift."

Years later, in 2012, Jim Bouton suffered a stroke that Michael says changed his dad's personality.

"My father would recognize his diminishing skills and it would become frustrating [for him] because he would know what he wanted to say, but he wouldn't be able to pull the words out. So, it's like things were going on and he was trapped. And then there was this underlying condition that ends up being related to dementia. It affects the blood vessels in the brain."

Michael last saw his father about two weeks before he died at home in 2019.

"My brother and I went up together, knowing it would be our last time seeing him. I'm a little sad that we passed on the opportunity to throw the ball. I know that if we had pushed him to do it, he would have thrown the ball, but I didn't want to push him. But what I did do—Dad used to do great imitations, and one of his imitations was of an elephant. His imitation was so good that when he went to the zoo, he would draw fire from the male elephants who would go on the warpath trying to figure out who was invading their turf.

"He wasn't so far gone that he didn't know what I was asking him to do. He knew I was asking him to do the elephant, and he did it."

In 2020, Mitchell Nathanson published a biography of Jim Bouton. Michael claims the author was unable to get the full picture of his father's life.

"He was forbidden [by step-mother Paula, according to Michael] from interviewing my brother and me as a condition of my father's assistance on the book. My mom [Bobbie] told me I wasn't allowed to be interviewed and how everyone else in the family knew that was the deal that was made."

In conversation, Michael details numerous other issues that he has with the relationship between his dad and stepmother, and with his own relationship with her. He says both impacted his relationship with his father, but he understands how it all happened.

"Regardless of my dad's flaws, this is shit that he did for love. When it comes down to it, my dad's biggest faults were the stupid things he did for love, and everyone does stupid shit for love."

Leo Cardenas and Leo Cardenas Jr.

"I Should Have Made It"

When we think of major league baseball players who hailed from Cuba, we tend to think of the more recent vintage stars, like Orlando Hernandez, Jose Abreu, and Aroldis Chapman, who defected from the island under dangerous, cloak-and-dagger circumstances. But in the years before the revolution that brought Fidel Castro to power, Cuba was a free-flowing pipeline of baseball talent to the United States. Among the stars making the journey were Luis Tiant, Tony Oliva, Tony Perez, Minnie Minoso, Bert Campaneris . . . and Leo Cardenas.

Cardenas was born in 1938, one of fifteen children of Rafael and Roberta Cardenas. He came to the United States in 1956 and played for the Tucson Cowboys in the Arizona-Mexico League for one season before signing a contract with the Cincinnati Redlegs in 1957 (from 1953 to 1959, the Cincinnati team was known as the Redlegs because of the negative connotation of "Reds" during the Joe McCarthy anti-communist era). In the pre-Castro days, the Redlegs actually had a triple-A minor league affiliate in Cuba, the Havana Sugar Kings, which played in the International League. Cardenas played shortstop for the Sugar Kings in 1960 following two seasons with Cincinnati's A-ball affiliate in Savannah.

During the 1960 season, Cardenas got the call to Cincinnati and made his major league debut against the Chicago Cubs on July 25. He played in "The Queen City" through the 1968 season, after which he was traded to the Minnesota Twins for a three-season stint before winding down his career with the California Angels, Cleveland Indians, and Texas Rangers from 1972 to 1975.

The right-handed hitter amassed 1,725 career hits and was a five-time all-star. He won a Gold Glove in 1965 for his defensive prowess at shortstop, which also earned him the nickname "Mr. Automatic." He was voted into the Reds Hall of Fame in 1981.

◆

Leo Cardenas Jr. was born in 1963, the third of five children—and only son—born to Gloria and Leo Cardenas. Leo Sr. was already an established major league player when Leo Jr. was in his formative years, which made for some difficult times.

"It really didn't dawn on me [that he was a baseball player]. I just knew that he would leave for spring training, but I didn't realize that's what he was doing. I would cry 'cause we all had to go to the airport and Dad was leaving."

Cardenas says the family lived in Cincinnati for the entirety of his father's career. Leo Jr. recalls the family's house as being "pretty big," and says that as the only boy he was able to have his own bedroom, while his sisters had to share.

"My dad was real funny. He wouldn't allow too many people into the house when he wasn't there. He was very protective like that. A lot of my friends were afraid to come over. But when my dad was at spring training they came over. Everybody was like, 'Oh, Mr. Cardenas is gone [laughs].'"

But when Leo Sr. was around, he would invite his friends over to the house.

"He would invite a lot of the ballplayers. We had a bunch of parties. My dad had a nice basement. Pete Rose, Tony Oliva, Rod Carew

. . . his friends, they'd come over a lot. They were just normal people to me. It's hard to explain. I never looked at them like, 'Oh God, they're this or that.' They were just people."

People whom Leo Jr. got to see up-close not only at home but at the ballpark as well.

"We went to the ballpark a lot when he was playing. I think my sisters were just kinda mad because I got to go into the clubhouse but they couldn't. So, in the clubhouse, man, you had all kinds of refreshments and candy, ice cream, you know what I'm saying? So, they were mad at me, but my dad made it up to them. He would

From the Cardenas family album: Leo Cardenas Jr. (foreground) at home with his family. *Leo Cardenas Jr.*

hand them stuff. And they understood. I think I was just being a brat and more or less just irritating them."

Young Leo reaped benefits beyond just candy and ice cream, although he didn't quite appreciate their significance at the time.

"Frank Robinson gave me a glove. He signed it. And I don't know what happened to that glove, man. He gave it to me when we were over his house in California. There's a Roberto Clemente bat that's supposed to be at our old house somewhere. We were hitting balls with it. In my second year of college, I was talking with Rod Carew, and he gave me one of his bats. Real skinny handle with a big old barrel on it. So, I'm in college and messing around taking batting practice with it. And the guy comes inside [with a pitch] and I kinda turned on it and I ended up breaking it. I was so pissed. Oh, my God. I about died."

At home, Leo Jr. did have an appreciation for his father's baseball paraphernalia, serving as an equipment manager of sorts.

"I shined his shoes and made sure his equipment was ready. Made sure his glove was ready, his shoes were clean, bat was ready. He would get these Louisville bats and I'd make sure they were ready to go and stuff like that. It was part of my chores."

Leo Jr. says his dad was the disciplinarian of the household.

"He ran a tight ship, man. I had sisters, you know, so he had to make sure there were no clowns coming around, that no one was messing with them or anything like that. He was always a strict dad. But he's alright, man."

Leo Jr. began developing a love for the game and major league aspirations of his own as a young boy.

"Dad would take me out in the yard many times. I'll never forget just having a toss with him and seeing, when he was throwing to me, how the ball would move. I mean, he really wasn't throwing that hard, but I was always like, 'My God, can I catch this?' He would make sure that I caught it, and as I got older, he would start 'bringing it' even more. I guess he was having me adjust to the speed. It helped me out. He was training my eyes to, you know, get me ready. So, later, whenever I'd see a guy throwing in the nineties, I'd say, 'Yeah, I got this.'

"We had a baseball diamond in our backyard. Not the actual measurements, but we had bases and a [pitcher's] mound, and we would play, all the [neighborhood] boys. Whenever I had a chance, I would grab about a dozen balls at the ballpark for us to play with. We all swung major league bats and played with major league balls."

Leo's parents divorced when young Leo was twelve, and he lived primarily with his mom from that point forward.

"That was tough because seeing him leave the house, I couldn't understand why this was going on. Why is this happening? And around that time, he stopped playing. I couldn't understand why. He was with Texas at the time. Billy Martin [the manager] kept calling, asking him to come back. And for some reason, you know, that was just his choice."

As his dad was hanging up his cleats, Leo Jr. was just getting started on what he hoped would be a professional baseball career of his own.

"People knew who I was, my name and everything. I grew up in Silverton [Ohio]. There were a lot of guys in my neighborhood who were really good all-around athletes. In high school, I was playing with Daryl Boston [who played in the major leagues 1984–1994]. Barry Larkin's dad had a Knothole Baseball team in Silverton called Stacey Moving & Storage. Barry was on the team, and his older brother Mike. We had a really, really good team, man. My dad would help out during the off-season. The story is that I was the shortstop and Barry Larkin was the second baseman [Barry Larkin went on to have a Hall of Fame career as a major league shortstop]. Everybody was good. I guess it motivated all the guys in the neighborhood to get better because we were all competing, and it drove us to get better."

Leo Jr. played shortstop and third base at Taft College in California. He signed with the Minnesota Twins organization as a fifteenth-round draftee in 1983.

Leo Jr. didn't mind when people compared him with his dad.

"It made me feel good. It made me want to get better. I mean, it was like, can I live up to that? My mom played a big role helping me through that by just believing in me. I knew I had big shoes to fill, but I knew I just had to focus on me and what I can do and what I can contribute. And I thought I should have made it. People thought I would and, even today, you know, I just wish—I should have made it."

With the Twins' Wisconsin Rapids (A-league) and Elizabethton (rookie league) teams in 1983, Leo Jr. batted .225 in 158 plate appearances.

"Mentally, it just wasn't there. I didn't prepare myself correctly. I let it slip through the cracks, and next thing you know, it was over with. I wasn't hurt, nothing like that. It was just my performance; I didn't produce. I was producing but I slacked off. I just slacked off, but I should have made it, man."

Today, Leo Jr. owns Leo's Handyman Co. in Cincinnati, and he occasionally performs maintenance work for Gateway Rehabilitation Hospital in Florence, Kentucky. He and his dad remain close (his mom died in 2017).

When Leo Sr. retired from baseball, he joined a slow-pitch softball league.

"They had a traveling team. It was big. He stopped playing major league baseball. But he continued to play [the game]. I mean, it was softball, but it was huge. And they respected my dad. He made everybody else better."

On a few occasions, Leo Jr. played alongside his dad when a fill-in player was needed.

"But I wasn't really into that because I was still playing hardball, man. Softball was too slow for me. I didn't want to mess up my timing."

Leo Jr. says that, over the years, his dad has given him a sense of what precipitated his journey to the United States.

"My dad and my uncle, his little brother, made it over here right before all that [the revolution] went down. My dad and mom had bought a house in Matanzas [Cuba]. And when all that went down, he had to leave, and Fidel seized all his stuff and his property. He had to leave all his stuff behind."

Initially, life wasn't so easy for Leo Sr. in the United States.

"He was in the minor leagues somewhere, Tucson or Laredo or something, and they had an incident where people were saying all kinds of racial stuff. And he mentioned that the KKK people said they were going to get him at the game. It was pretty rough having to deal with that. You're there to play baseball."

In the early years of his career, Leo Sr. regularly sent money back home to his family in Cuba.

"I think one of his sisters told him, 'Hey, stop sending money because the government is taking it.' So, he stopped sending the money. I have a bunch of cousins who are still there. We communicate with one of them through Facebook."

The two Leos live near each other in Ohio and see each other often.

"We go fishing a lot. We went recently and he was trying to pull in a big fish. He couldn't even bend down. I was afraid he'd fall in. I was trying to hold him, trying to grab him. But I think I grabbed him too hard. He said, 'Oh man, you can't be grabbing me like that!' [laughs]. One day I was up at one of the lakes he goes to. I went up to see how he was doing. And a guy says, 'Your dad fell into the lake trying to grab a fish' [laughs]. You know what, though? He's a true fisherman."

16

Bobby Richardson and Robby Richardson

Getting Past Frank Crosetti, Baseball Cop

With the likes of Mickey Mantle, Yogi Berra, Roger Maris, Whitey Ford, and Elston Howard, the great New York Yankees teams of the mid-fifties to mid-sixties had no shortage of star power. Still, one could make an argument that the steady rock of those teams was the 5-9, 170-pound second baseman, Bobby Richardson.

The Sumter, South Carolina, native made his major league debut as a nineteen-year-old in the summer of 1955 and played for the Yankees, and only the Yankees, until retiring at age thirty-one after the 1966 season.

Richardson was remarkably durable. He surpassed 700 plate appearances four times, 600 appearances another two times, and 500 appearances two times. He led the American League in at-bats three times and in base hits, with 209, in 1962. In that season, Richardson made 754 plate appearances and struck out only twenty-four times. He finished second to Mickey Mantle that year in the voting for Most Valuable Player, one of six seasons in which Richardson garnered MVP votes. He won five Gold Glove Awards and was voted to eight American League All-Star teams.

As steady as he was during the regular season, Richardson took his game to another level in the World Series.

In 1960, when the Yankees lost in seven games to the Pittsburgh Pirates, Richardson batted .367 (eleven hits in thirty at-bats), with twelve runs batted in and an on-base + slugging percentage of 1.054. In game three of the series, he hit a grand slam home run en route to the only six-RBI World Series game in the twentieth century. He was voted MVP of the series, the first—and still the only—World Series MVP from the losing team.

The following year, Richardson hit .391 (9–23) in a five-game World Series win over the Cincinnati Reds.

In 1962, Richardson caught a bullet line drive off the bat of Willie McCovey with runners on second and third and two outs in the bottom of the ninth of game seven, preserving a 1–0 win and World Championship for New York.

In the 1964 World Series, which the Yankees lost in seven games to the St. Louis Cardinals, Richardson batted .406 (13–32). His thirteen hits remain the fourth most in World Series history. Remarkably, seven of the thirteen hits came off one of the greatest World Series pitchers of all time, Hall of Famer Bob Gibson.

For his career, Richardson batted .305 across seven World Series, thirty-nine points higher than his career average in the regular season, despite facing a steady stream of premier pitching in high-pressure circumstances.

The Yankees recognized Richardson's contributions to the franchise's success with a Bobby Richardson Day at Yankee Stadium on September 17, 1966, in advance of his already-announced retirement at season's end.

A few years after retiring from major league baseball, Richardson accepted the head coaching position for the University of South Carolina's baseball team. He was the Gamecocks' first full-time coach and dedicated himself to putting SC baseball on the map. And that he did, leading the team to three NCAA tournament appearances, including a trip to the College World Series championship game in 1975. When he stepped down in 1976, he was celebrated as

"The Father of South Carolina Baseball." He was inducted into the school's Hall of Fame in 2004, and into the state of South Carolina Hall of Fame in 1996.

Richardson is a devout Southern Baptist who was asked to speak at the funerals of several former teammates, including that of Mickey Mantle in 1995.

◆

Like his father, Robby Richardson was a lead-off hitter of sorts as the first of five children—three boys and two girls—born to Betsy and Bobby Richardson.

The Richardson family's home was in Sumter, South Carolina, but they would spend the summers in the leafy suburb of Ridgewood, New Jersey, about a forty-five-minute ride to the Bronx.

"We would rent a house in Ridgewood. My mom had a cousin who lived in Ridgewood and helped us find a house the first year. We enjoyed the community and came back to it every year. We'd rent a house for the summer months. Dad would play catch with us in the yard, or he'd throw us a Wiffle Ball, that type of thing.

"There were a number of ballplayers that were there, or in neighboring areas, and so lots of times Dad would carpool with several of the players. I remember stories of him going in with [Jim] Bouton, Yogi [Berra], Steve Hamilton [a relief pitcher].

"Being the oldest of five, I was the one that was able to go to the stadium a pretty good bit with him. It's hard for me to believe that, at seven, Dad used to take me with him into the stadium and I'd be in the dugout, in the clubhouse before the game, be with him there until they went out for batting practice. And then he'd send me up into the stands by myself and said in the ninth inning, come to this door, meet me right here. So, I'd spend the day by myself in Yankee Stadium. Same usher every time; people got to know the family. I think that's the reason Dad was comfortable with my being there by myself.

"If you walked up to the back of the lower section, there was a policeman guarding a door to some stairs that went down. I used to call it the family room. It was an area down on the same concourse as the clubhouse and they had a closed-circuit television in there. And so, as soon as the eighth inning was over, Dad would say, okay, come down. I don't know how many games I saw in Yankee Stadium, fifty or sixty or whatever, but I never saw the ninth inning [laughs]. Dad would come off the field, shower and we could beat the traffic. Back in those days, they didn't have to have press availability. The reporters would go to the locker of whoever they wanted to talk to. And it was seldom Dad [laughs]. So, he could shower, grab me in the family room, and hit the car and we'd get across the George Washington Bridge in front of the traffic. Dad always said that he knew that if he got a [big] hit late in the ballgame, that he was going to be late going across the bridge [laughs]."

The family car in those days was a Jeep Wagoneer.

"Dad and Mel Stottlemyre [a Yankee pitcher] met the vice president of the Willys Company, who made a Jeep station wagon called the Wagoneer. So, this executive would get a brand new one and drive it for a year and then he would sell it to Mel one year and Dad the next."

Robby has fond memories of his time in the clubhouse.

"There were a couple of players, [Roger] Maris or [Clete] Boyer or somebody, they all called me 'Little Rich.' I was pretty good friends with a lot of them. I was very good friends with 'Big Pete' and 'Little Pete,' Pete Sheehy and Pete Previte, the two clubhouse guys. I used to get frisked by [third base coach] Frank Crosetti just about once a week. His locker was right by the door. One of the things with 'Cro' back in those days was he didn't want people taking baseballs. He was kind of the self-appointed ball police. Big Pete would always put out a big box of Bazooka bubblegum, the old little rectangular squares. And I'd take a handful of that when I was going up into the stands. Pete knew it, but it looked like a baseball in my pocket. And

Crosetti would stop me all the time to make sure it wasn't a baseball that I was taking out of the clubhouse [laughs]."

Bobby Richardson's devout religious beliefs were well known by his teammates, which sometimes led to amusing situations.

"All of his teammates knew who Dad was and what he stood for. I was very good friends with Moose [Skowron, a former teammate of Bobby's] towards the end of his life. And Moose always used to tell me the story about coming in after striking out and he would come down the dugout and be like [makes grumbling sounds], and then he'd get to Dad and he'd say, 'Sorry, Rich.' My daughter, Amy, had heard that story. I took her to a game in Chicago when the Yankees were playing and Moose was doing a public relations job for the White Sox. I bought the tickets off of StubHub or something. And I sent a note up to him and he came down and he was like, 'How the blank did you—sorry, Amy—get these tickets? How the blank—sorry, Amy.' So, she felt like she was part of the club after that [laughs].

"When I was probably about three, I was coming down into the clubhouse with Dad after a game and, I don't know all the details, but I've heard the story from both Dad and Hank [Bauer, a former Yankee] and from some other people. Hank, in a joking manner, opened a beer, handed it to me as a three-year-old, and said, 'Here, take a drink of this, it'll put hair on your chest.' And Dad knocked it out of Hank's hand and my hand, and it skittered across the floor. And they say the whole place just went silent. Hank Bauer was a marine, just as tough as they get. And Hank apologized to Dad. Towards the end of Hank's life, they were doing one of those Yankees fantasy camps. And Dad called me two days before it started and said, 'Hank wants to know if you can come down. Can you put a uniform on and just fill in for these guys?' The guys still want to bat, but they didn't want to play in the field. So, when I went to fly out, I went to the airport with Hank Bauer, Don Larsen, and Moose Skowron. It must have been 7:30 in the morning. There was an old guy with a Yankee hat sweeping the floor. He looked up, he said, 'You're Hank Bauer! And you're Don Larsen! And you're Moose Skowron!' And he looked at me and said, 'Who the blank are you?' Moose got all upset. Hank called me over to the side, and he said, 'Robby, I need to ask you a question. Are you the one I tried to give the beer to?' And I said I am. And he said, 'You know, I didn't mean anything by it.' He was apologizing to me for something that happened forty-something years before."

Among the many kids of Yankee players, Robby was particularly close to one.

"The [player's son] that I was closest to during those days was Ellie [Howard] Jr. He and I would sit together in the stands a lot and talk and watch the game, that type of thing. Back then, the only ice cream they served in the stadium was a little cup with vanilla, strawberry, and chocolate. Ellie Jr. really liked strawberry. I liked chocolate. We'd throw away the vanilla [laughs].

"I got to know the other Yankee kids mostly in spring training when we would go to Florida for six weeks. The Yankees had an arrangement with a private school; basically, it was a one-room schoolhouse. They'd send a bus to pick up some of us. They had two teachers that were in there like as private tutors. We'd bring our assignments from the schools in South Carolina, Missouri, wherever it was, and get in our 180 days. So, I was always riding the bus with the Maris kids and the [Mickey] Mantle kids, the [Whitey] Ford kids."

Spring training and regular-season games were the extent of Robby's in-person Yankee experiences.

"I never got to go to a World Series because it was always during school time. I have very clear memories of '63 and '64. Our school got out at 2:30, but in those days the World Series games started at 1 o'clock. Teachers would say, 'Your dad got a hit in the first inning off [Bob] Gibson.' They'd be listening on the radio.

"I knew Dad was more in the public eye than the parents of my other friends. I don't think I ever resented it. Dad was always so gracious with people. People would come up and he'd stop and take time to talk to them. He felt that it was part and parcel of what he did for a living. And it just became part of being out [with him]. I think he enjoys giving other people a chance to spend time, not to feel like they're just hurriedly getting a signature."

In today's game, a player like Bobby Richardson would be able to retire as a multi-millionaire. That was not the case in the pre–free agency era of Richardson's day, when most players had to find off-season jobs to make ends meet.

"His first couple of years [with the Yankees] he worked in a gas station, pumping gas, doing those types of things. So, after the 1960 season, it would have been the World Series MVP that was filling your car up with gas! Later, the YMCA started offering him a job during the off-season to work with kids. So, he always had an off-season job until maybe the last couple of years toward the end of his career. The Yankees were trying to talk him out of retiring and they would offer more and more money to have him come back. I did the math; he was basically paid $33 a game his first couple of years in New York. The minimum salary was $5,000 and you played 154 games a year. The biggest percentage raise he ever got was when the minimum salary went from $5,000 to $7,000.

"[Dad] was going to retire at the end of the '64 season. He and Tony [shortstop Tony Kubek] were both going to step down. They decided to play one more year, and at the end of the '65 season, they were both going to step down. But the Yankees had Bobby Murcer coming up and they wanted one of the two players to stay and play with Murcer to kind of break him in. At that time, Murcer was a shortstop. It was all arranged. Tony was going to play, and Dad was going to step down after '65. And then Tony went to the Mayo Clinic. When he was in the reserves in '62, he pinched a nerve in his shoulder and the Mayo Clinic told him that if he kept playing, he risked further health problems. And so, that's why he retired at the end of '65. And the Yankees came to Dad and said, it was kind of a gentleman's agreement that they wouldn't both step down. And so, he played for actually two more years than he wanted to. He loved baseball, but just was tired of being away from family."

Robby played baseball throughout his childhood.

"I loved baseball. When I was in high school, I played every sport. I don't know that I used to have a day off. In three years of high school, I earned ten letters in six different sports. Baseball was my favorite, and I was pretty good at it. I always joke with people—half joke, half true—they'd say, 'Of course you were a good ballplayer, you had a major league dad to teach you.' And I'd say, 'No, he was always gone. Mom taught us everything we know about baseball.' And then I'd follow-up by saying, 'But that was all right, she was a better athlete than he was [laughs].' That's not necessarily true, but Mom would get out with us and do a lot of that playing.

"I played high school and college ball. I played one year for Dad at the University of South Carolina and then ended up transferring to a smaller school in Indiana. I was only at [SC] for one semester. Dad came to me and said, 'Robby, I'm going to step down. Your scholarship is fine. You can stay for the next three years, or if you want to, go somewhere else.' I had wrestled with going to a smaller Christian college or playing for him. Really, the only reason I was there was to play for Dad. I loved playing for him, loved the way he thought about the game. So, I chose to transfer.

"My best position was outfield. I played shortstop in high school and at the small college, but my best position would have been outfield. But I knew at best I was going to be a double-A ballplayer, and I knew enough about minor league baseball to know that wasn't the direction that I wanted to go."

In American Legion ball one night while in high school, Robby had a couple of prominent fans drop in on his game in Sumter.

"I was getting dressed in my uniform, ready to go out to the game and the doorbell rang and it was Roger and Pat Maris. They had just dropped their boys off at a golf camp in Pinehurst, North Carolina, were driving back to Florida, and saw 'Sumter' on the interstate and said, 'Hey, we have to pull off and see if we can find the Richardsons' house.' And they came by and Dad talked them into staying and going to the American Legion game that night."

In Sumter, fans were kind to Robby. Not so much on the road, though.

"In Sumter, everybody knew Dad, so there was not any kind of negative jab to it. On the road, I'd hear some of that. 'You can't hit the curveball like your dad,' that type of stuff. It really never bothered me or put that much pressure on me."

After college, Robby entered the ministry.

"Part of it was following Dad's footsteps, part of it was just where I felt I could make the most impact. I spent a lot of time doing different things. I've worked with youth in the church, spent some time as a pastor, headed up a Christian conference center for a couple of years, worked with a communications ministry for thirteen years."

Bobby Richardson was invited to give the prayer of dedication at the renovated Yankee Stadium when it opened in April 1976.

"George Steinbrenner asked him to come up, so I flew up with Dad. I remember [Yankee catcher] Thurman Munson called Dad over and we sat by his locker. Thurman said that you [Bobby] got out of baseball early because of your family and I'm wrestling with the same thing. He was considering stepping out because of his family. And that's why he bought the plane, so he could go home on days off and spend more time with his family."

Munson was killed when the plane he was piloting crashed on August 2, 1979, in Akron, Ohio. The Yankee captain had flown home on an off-day to be with his family.

Another interaction with Yankee players leaves a more humorous memory.

"My daughter, Amy, lived and taught in Boston for a while. She rented a room from the community relations director of the Red Sox. The Yankees played at Fenway the first game of the season and she asked Amy if [my] dad would come up for a Jimmy Fund event. That's their fundraiser for kids. Dad said he would do it. They gave Dad and Amy on-field passes for before the game. I told Amy, I said, 'Look, the one thing you need to know about Dad is, he's going to want to leave early, so just roll with it.' So, they had really good seats and Amy called me that night and said, 'I know you said he wanted to leave early, but at the end of the second inning?!' [laughs].

"I think it's just one of those things after playing in 1,500 or whatever games, he enjoys being around the game, but just sitting there watching didn't interest him."

In 2018, Robby and his dad attended the Yankees' annual Old Timers' Day in New York.

"I was standing around afterwards. They had a suite for the [Old Timers]. And Willie Randolph [former Yankee second baseman] came up to me and said, 'Robby, I know your dad is getting to the point that he has you come in and do logistics. If you ever can't come, just call me. I'll pick up your dad at the airport.' I walked away and Ron Guidry [former Yankee pitcher] called me over to the side and said, 'Look, if your dad's coming into town and you ever need somebody to pick him up. . . .' It was just one of those [nice] things to see ballplayers saying here's how much we think of your dad."

Another measure of the high regard in which Richardson was held by his teammates is in the number of eulogies he has given for his former colleagues.

"He did the message at Mickey's. Bob Costas did the eulogy and Dad did the message. He's done—I can't name them all—Bob Turley, Ralph Houk, Steve Hamilton, Jim Coates, Moose Skowron, Clete Boyer, Art Ditmar. He considers it an honor."

Robby is remembered fondly, too.

"It was the last day of the season in 1987 or '88. I was asked to speak at Yankee Stadium for a chapel service for the Yankees and Orioles. It was a cold day and I had on a heavy coat and a sweater. I walked up to the door of the Yankee clubhouse and was fumbling for my press pass and the policeman sitting there said, 'You don't need that, I know who you are. I've been here for forty years.' And he called me Butterball. That was Big Pete's nickname for me. And he called over another policeman. The other policeman said, 'Little Rich, what are you doing here?' That's like twenty years [after his dad retired]. Those are good memories for me."

About twenty-five years later, the Yankees were commemorating the fiftieth anniversary of Roger Maris's season of sixty-one home runs in 1961. Maris had passed away some years earlier, but his wife, Pat, was there along with her kids.

"Danny and David [Mantle] came up. On the way out to the ballpark, the Yankees provided a double-decker bus. I was up on top and sat down to talk to Kevin [Maris], who's a dead ringer for Roger, and

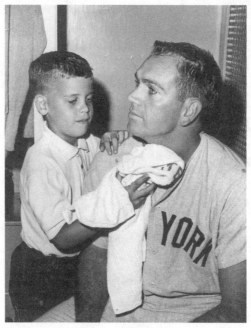

Robby Richardson towels off his dad after a tough road game. *Robby Richardson*

David Mantle, who's a dead ringer for his dad. And I look a lot like Dad. So, Kevin and David, and I were sitting around a table at the top of the bus and Pat Maris came up from the spiral stairway and just stopped and gasped. She said she had a flashback, you know, to see the three players sitting together."

Today, Robby Richardson and his wife live in Muskegon, Michigan, and he manages a kitchen store called Kneaded Kitchens. They raised a son and twin girls, and his dad, once known as Rich by his teammates, is now called pop-pop by his grandchildren.

"As I look back on it now, I'm very grateful. It's an unusual way to grow up, with a dad in the public eye, and with all that's going on with that. I don't look back with any regrets. Dad grew up quail hunting in South Carolina and quail season runs from Thanksgiving Day through March 1, basically the off-season. So, we would spend time hunting together, fishing together, those types of things. When he was around, he maximized his time with us. There's probably a sense in which the girls didn't have quite the same experience. Dad knew what to do with boys. I don't think he had the same comfort level with daughters. So, he would buy things for them and spend time with us.

"I mean, it was hard with Dad being gone that much. You know, there were things that were tough, but Dad and Mom always made it the best they could."

Mike Hargrove and Andy Hargrove

Fishing off Bo Jackson's Lap

Mike Hargrove carved out two distinctive and highly successful careers in the major leagues.

Fans who grew up in the 1990s and aughts know him as manager of the Cleveland Indians (now known as the Guardians), Baltimore Orioles, and Seattle Mariners. He was particularly successful in Cleveland, leading the club to five consecutive American League Central Division titles from 1995 to 1999, a run that included World Series appearances in 1995 and 1997. He compiled a 721–591 record in Cleveland, good for a winning percentage of .550 and a ranking of third on the team's all-time winningest manager list, trailing only Terry Francona and Lou Boudreau. Overall, Hargrove won 1,188 games as a big league manager from 1991 to 2007.

Fans of an earlier generation remember Hargrove as a patient, left-hand-hitting first baseman who was one of the toughest outs in baseball. The twenty-fifth-round draft pick of the Texas Rangers compiled a batting average of .290 and an on-base percentage of .396 across twelve seasons with Texas (1974–1978), the San Diego Padres (1979), and Cleveland (1979–1985). He was named American League Rookie of the Year in 1974, when he batted .323, and was an All-Star the following season. He hit over .300 in six seasons, had 100+ walks four times, and led the American League in on-base percentage (.424) in 1981.

He was inducted into the Indians Hall of Fame in 2008 and the Greater Cleveland Sports Hall of Fame in 2013. He also was inducted into the Hall of Fame of his alma mater, Northwestern Oklahoma State University, and had his number retired by the school in 2007. In 1999, Hargrove was inducted into the National Association of Intercollegiate Sports (NAIA) Hall of Fame.

Mike Hargrove also possesses one of baseball's all-time great nicknames: The Human Rain Delay. This was a well-earned moniker, as Hargrove would step out of the batter's box to adjust his batting gloves, tap his helmet, hike up his pants, bang the dirt out of his cleats with his bat, and dig himself a toehold. After. Every. Pitch. Needless to say, he drove pitchers crazy, particularly after he would follow his routine with one of his patented line drives into the gap.

Mike Hargrove's baseball journey is the very definition of the phrase "a baseball life." In an August 5, 2008, story in the online *Cleveland Magazine*, Hargrove said that he and his wife, Sharon, had moved at least a hundred times during his thirty-five years in professional baseball, living in twenty-three cities in thirteen states.

◆

Andrew Hargrove is from the later generation of baseball fans mentioned above who remember his dad primarily as a major league manager. Andy was born in Cleveland in October 1981, shortly after his father's third of seven seasons playing for the Indians. He was the fourth of five children, the only boy.

"Up until, I think it was '93, we would live wherever Dad was, whether it was Batavia [New York] or Williamsport [Pennsylvania], or Colorado Springs [Colorado] when he went back to the minor leagues to try to make it back up as a coach. And the rest of the year, during the winter, we'd live in Perryton, Texas, where my parents were from and had a house.

"It was always great to go back home because you knew what you had. You knew your friends and your surroundings. Our first years in Cleveland [when Andy's father was managing the Indians] were tough. It always seemed that our spring break in Texas and the spring break in Cleveland were kind of back-to-back. So, we'd go to spring training for two weeks and then we'd get back into town [Cleveland], and I'd be going to school with a bunch of kids that had been going to school with each other since September.

"But I'm a big believer that all those different situations have molded us to be the people we are and to give us the ability to talk to anybody and try to relate as much as possible. So, those earlier years, where you're going into a new situation and it was always a little bit difficult, probably had to do more with being shy and wanting to belong."

When his dad played for and later managed the Indians, the Hargrove family lived in Strongsville, Ohio, a suburb of Cleveland. When Andy was sixteen or so, the family moved to Richfield, Ohio, a small village located about halfway between Cleveland and Akron.

"They [his parents] just wanted a little bit more land to kind of make it feel a bit more like Perryton, with tons of trees and stuff like that."

It was also a setting that was far removed from the pressures of the ballpark.

"Dad did a great job of always leaving baseball at the ballpark, not bringing home frustrations. Sometimes his coaches would come by the house for dinner. I remember Sunday night dinners with his third base coach, Jeff Newman, and his pitching coach, Rick Adair, who had two younger kids and we'd play baseball all the time."

Andy often went to the ballpark with his dad.

"I'd have hitting lessons with Brian Graham, who was one of my dad's coaches. I'd play catch with [players] Kenny Lofton and Carlos Baerga and Albert Belle. And [pitcher] Bud Black taught me how to stop getting on the side of the ball. I can remember playing catch with him a couple of hours before batting practice. We'd be on the left field line, and we'd play catch. And if I accidentally got on the side of the ball, he'd let it go by. And so, at the beginning, there would be 120 balls out there that I had to go pick up. Those things were normal to me. Looking back now, it's pretty incredible. It's a pretty good way to grow up and learn the game."

A bit earlier in his life, Andy had a couple of particularly interesting experiences.

"Dad [managed] in the Instructional League one year, and the Royals had a player there, Bo Jackson. And I went fishing with him and sat on his lap. I mean, it's Bo Jackson . . . that's crazy! Another time, in 1994, when they opened Jacobs Field [now Progressive Field], President Clinton came to throw out the first pitch. I'm [wearing] this dirty pine tar batting glove and I'm shaking the president of the United States' hand. I was thirteen, and I had an opportunity to warm him up before the game. But I guess I got too scared with all the secret service all over the place, so I missed out on [doing it]."

A frequent pastime of Andy's was taking cuts in the batting cages underneath the stands while the game was going on.

"I'd be down there the majority of the time. If not, I'd be in Dad's office watching the game, or in the stands. I had the rules laid out to me that I couldn't get in the way of the players. Once the game was on, if they came in I needed to get out of their way. And then I did what I could to make sure I was out of Dad's way once the game was over so he could get his media obligations out of the way, get his conversations done with the players or the front office. But the majority of the time I was trying to hone my own craft."

When Andy rode home with his dad after the games, there was little baseball talk in the car—at least between father and son.

"He might kill me for telling you this, but he would listen to post-game shows on the ride home. He wouldn't talk about it, but he listened. I always found that interesting because when I got old enough to have my own opinions, I don't know how [he] could stand it. It drove me crazy. [He] obviously had thicker skin than me."

Unlike sports radio hosts and callers, Andy never questioned his father about his managerial moves.

"Dad always has been [my] idol. You kind of trust what your parents do. Until you get to a certain age, and then you question every single thing they say [laughs]. The only time I ever questioned his expertise was anytime he was trying to teach me [how to play]. I mean, it's such a father-son thing. I have a funny story about that. It was spring training. The players don't generally show up until seven-thirty, eight o'clock in the morning. But we'd go to the ballpark at like five in the morning. And Brian [Graham] would throw me batting practice in the cages for like an hour. And [one day] I went into Dad's office and I'm like, 'Dad, Brian knows everything about hitting. It's unbelievable.' And my dad goes, 'Andy, shut the door.' And so, I shut the door. He goes, 'Where do you think he learned it? Brian knows a ton about baseball, but I've been telling you the same stuff for years and you don't listen.' It's funny now, being a father and I'm actually seeing the other side of it."

Despite his dad's ability to leave the game at the ballpark, there was still plenty of baseball talk around the Hargrove household.

"The baseball talk was centered around the good with the Indians, and how my games were going. I was fortunate that I was able to get into a good organization summer ball–wise. By the time I was fourteen or fifteen, I was playing eighteen and under, playing sixty to eighty games a summer, and another thirty during the fall. So, with him being on the road half the time, he wanted to hear about what was going on with me."

During the winter months, Andy got to see his dad a lot more, especially once the family moved to Ohio year-round.

"When we lived in Texas, if Dad needed to come to Cleveland or needed to go to the winter meetings or whatever, he'd be gone for a week. So, when we moved to Cleveland, he was around a lot more. A

Andy Hargrove with his dad in 1986. *Gaines-DuVall Sports Portraits and Sharon Hargrove*

really neat memory was, I think it was Fox 8 news, [Dad] was doing an interview. It was during the winter, and they sent a limo and we all went to dinner at this place called Johnny's in Cleveland and then we took the limo to Fox 8. Me and my sisters, we thought we were pretty cool. This was around the time when those Grey Poupon commercials were on [the commercials prominently featured an aristocrat in a limo]. I remember that being a prevalent joke that night."

Was it difficult being out in public with his dad?

"No. There were times when we were trying to eat dinner, you know, 'Can we just eat?' kind of thing. But I remember how excited people were. And I always thought it was a pretty neat deal that everybody wants to talk to him and pick his brain and get an autograph from him.

"I liken it this way: My son, unfortunately, wasn't able to be around the things that I was around as a kid. When he was four or five, we went out to Arizona to see my parents and he was a huge fan of Nick Swisher [a Cleveland outfielder/first baseman]. And so, we went up to Goodyear [in Arizona, where the Indians held spring training] from Tucson one day and Dad talked to—I think it was Tito [Terry] Francona—to ask him if we could just kind of walk around. Dad, he's a part of the organization, but I think he still wanted to make sure that he's not stepping on any toes or anything like that. But seeing the look that my son had on his face when he saw Nick Swisher and [Indians players] Michael Brantley, Jason Kipnis, and Michael Bourn, it reminded me of the times [I was out with my dad and people got excited to see him]."

Andy harbored pro baseball ambitions of his own.

"That was my goal. I jokingly say this and it's partially true, but in college, I was an athlete-student. I wasn't a student-athlete as I should have been. I went to school so I could play.

"I remember those days of playing catch with [Dad] and he'd throw me pop-ups, or us going to a batting cage. I'm sure it would be like my son wanting me to sell elevators on my days off [Andy is a modernization sales rep for Otis, the elevator and escalator manufacturer]. But, he always did it.

"When I was younger, I didn't listen as much as I should [to his father's baseball advice]. As I got older, I realized, 'Oh, I've got one of the better baseball minds in the world here. Maybe I should listen a little bit.' When I got to high school, probably my junior or senior year, is really when we would talk about things. In, I think it was my sophomore year of college, I went to Baltimore, and we sat down and went through my thought process at the plate and what my approach needed to be for that season. I think I still have the paper that he wrote it down on. It was on 'From the Desk of Mike Hargrove' with the Orioles logo on it. And I had an amazing year. I think I hit like .420; I was third in the nation in home runs."

Was there added pressure being the son of a well-known major league player and successful manager?

"I don't think I ever had any pressure when I was playing. I was a good player. When I was at St. Ignatius [a Cleveland high school], I made varsity my freshman year. I was the second person to do that in school history. I remember getting a question from a news reporter on camera: How did I feel about people thinking the only reason I was on varsity baseball was because of who my dad was? So, I'm sure those thoughts were out there. It's just human nature."

After high school, Andy was selected by the Baltimore Orioles in the thirty-first round of the 2000 amateur draft. He didn't sign, choosing instead to enroll in junior college before attending Oral Roberts University for one year and then one year at Kent State University. He graduated from Kent and was selected in the forty-seventh round by the Seattle Mariners in the 2005 amateur draft.

"Now, [were] there things that benefitted me from Dad being who he was? Absolutely. I mean, in my senior year of college, I didn't have a great year, but I got the opportunity to play professional baseball and that's because of who my dad was and how the organization felt about him. And I was able to turn it into three years."

Andy played in the Seattle minor league system from 2005 to 2007, topping out at the Double-A level.

"I was talking to my dad, maybe a couple of years ago. I said, 'I always wonder what if I had just signed out of high school, because by the time I [actually] got into professional baseball it would have been my fifth year of pro baseball, instead of my first. And Dad put it into perspective. He said, 'Think about your life. If you did that, you wouldn't know Laura [Andy's wife]. You wouldn't have your kids. It could be totally different.' And that really made me think. I mean, if you ask the eighteen-year-old me, I probably would have told you I wanted to [go into pro ball]. Thank goodness that's not what I did, and I was able to get my degree and still get to live my dream and play professional baseball. I got paid to do it for three years. Not too many people in the world get to say they got paid to do what they love to do. So, I'll take it."

Dad's support was instrumental in Andy being able to live his dream for three years.

"Every level you go, the game just gets a little quicker. It's just a little more crisp. After the first day, I called my dad and I'm like, 'I can't do this. I'm in the wrong place. I'm stealing someone's spot.' I was overwhelmed. I was intimidated. And he said, 'You're not stealing anyone's spot. You gotta stick it out. You're good enough. You can do this.' I went the next day and I had calmed down. It was just baseball, right? It's a little quicker, but I realized, 'Okay, I can do this.' And I ended up being an Arizona League All-Star that year."

The question that must be asked: Was Andy Hargrove a Human Rain Delay Jr.?

"No, no [laughs]. It's funny, every single time I got interviewed when I was in high school, college, and professional baseball that would come up. But no, I couldn't do that."

But, Mike Hargrove fans can take solace in the fact that some things never change.

"We were golfing. This was a couple or three years back. And Dad kind of does this thing when he's about to hit his drive. He just, sometimes he'll take like eight swings, and I'm like, 'Let's go! Get in there, hit it . . . let's go!' [laughs]."

Andy was released by the Mariners in 2007.

"When I got released, I kind of went, 'Oh, what do I do? I've never thought this far.' I ended up getting a sales job, but it wasn't the right situation. But [former Indians player] Joe Charboneau was an instructor at a baseball facility in Brecksville, Ohio, and he said, 'You should come up and give lessons.' I did that for two, two-and-a-half years. I worked a day job and then I'd go give lessons at night, before we had kids. And right before we decided to have kids, I sent out my resume to all the teams trying to get an interview to coach. But it was probably a bit too late; I want to say it was like January. And then my wife and I decided to start our family. And I just felt that with the [small] amount of money you start off making in the minor leagues as a coach, she wouldn't be able to travel 'cause we wouldn't be able to afford to live.

"So, I ended up finding a sales job that's led me to where I am now [at Otis]. And I couldn't be happier with the fact that I'm home every night and get to coach my son.

"I do wish that my kids could see and live the life that I was fortunate enough to grow up in. But they do get to see little peeks of it because we get to go to the games quite often with Dad still being part of the [organization]. And my son is getting to the age where he asks questions about Kenny Lofton, Jim Thome, Carlos Baerga . . . so, him asking me questions about playing catch with Jim Thome, it kind of takes me back. It was normal for me then, and now I think about it and I'm like, 'That's pretty neat.'"

Mike Hargrove is senior advisor to Chris Antonetti, the Cleveland Guardians' president, Baseball Operations. But he also carries another important title: Papa [grandpa].

"He's a little less strict on them [Andy and Laura's three children—one boy and two girls] than he was us. He's the same way to them, though, in that he's always kinda got a joking manner about some of [their] questions. I mean, he was a great manager, right? What's being a parent or grandparent? It's coaching, coaching people through life. Out of fifteen grandkids [including the children of Andy's sisters] there are four boys. The Hargroves, we don't get too many boys. But it's really neat to see him talk to them when it comes to baseball or when they're getting a little too rough, all the young ones around. They'll listen to him. He has a commanding presence. He loves the kids to death."

Mike and Sharon Hargrove now live in Tucson for a good part of the year, returning to Ohio for the summer.

"During the summer, we see them a lot. We generally go over to their house for Sunday dinner. We hang out on their patio. Sunday has always been a big family day. I remember growing up that we weren't allowed to do anything on Sundays with our friends."

For the Hargroves, it's always been about family.

"My mom has this map in their suite at Progressive Field [where the Guardians play in Cleveland] that has a pin in it for everywhere they lived, and it's just incredible. And she did everything to make sure that our family was together, that we ate dinner together and that when Dad was home, we were a family. Never did it ever feel like it was crazy. It was normal. It really is impressive what she's done, and what she continues to do."

Andy laughingly offers a suggestion for the title of this book, one that perhaps best sums up the vagabond existence, crazy hours, memorable characters, and wild memories that all comprise the typical baseball life: "Idiots of Baseball."

18

Ron Guidry and Brandon Guidry

Handfuls of Bazooka and Other Stadium Fun

At 5-11 and 161 pounds, Ron Guidry was not a particularly imposing figure on the pitcher's mound. Until, that is, he unleashed a blazing fastball and devasting slider, the latter learned under the tutelage of teammate Sparky Lyle, which earned Guidry the nickname "Louisiana Lightning."

To understand the Lafayette, Louisiana, native's dominance for the New York Yankees in the late 1970s and early 1980s, one can compare his won-lost record to that of another left-hander, Hall of Famer Sandy Koufax, who is acknowledged as one of the most dominant pitchers of all time. The Dodger great was 165–87 in his career, a winning percentage of .655. Guidry was 170–91, .651.

Guidry was a three-time twenty-game winner whose 1978 season stands as one of the greatest ever. He went 25–3 that year (.893 winning percentage) with an earned run average of 1.74. He tied an American League record with nine shutouts, led the league in WHIP (walks + hits per inning pitched) with a 0.94 mark, and allowed only 187 hits in almost 274 innings pitched. He set a Yankee record that still stands when he struck out eighteen California Angels at Yankee Stadium on June 17. He went 2–0 that postseason, helping the Yankees to a World Series win over the Los Angeles Dodgers. He was the unanimous winner of the AL Cy Young Award and finished second to Jim Rice of the Boston Red Sox in the Most Valuable Player voting.

In addition to being a three-time twenty-game winner, "Gator" was a four-time all-star and winner of five Gold Gloves for fielding prowess. He was a two-time World Series champion who compiled a 3–1 record in the Fall Classic with a 1.69 ERA. In addition to winning the Cy Young Award in 1978, Guidry finished in the top five in the voting three other times. He won fifteen or more games six times.

Guidry, a third-round draft pick by the Yankees out of the University of Louisiana at Lafayette, played his entire career (1975–1988) for New York. He served as Yankees co-captain (with second baseman Willie Randolph) from 1986 to 1988, and his uniform number, 49, was retired by the team in 2003, only the second Yankees pitcher, after Whitey Ford, to be so honored.

Following his playing days, Guidry served as Yankees pitching coach under manager Joe Torre in 2006 and 2007.

Today, he is a retired grandfather living with his wife, Bonnie, in Lafayette.

◆

Brandon Guidry was born in May 1980 in Lafayette but has chosen to make New York City his home.

"My whole family still lives in Louisiana on what we would like to call a compound. My parents have like seventy-five acres of land. And what you'd do in the South is, you give your children an acre here, an acre there. So, my older sister lives right next door [to my parents]. My younger sister is probably going to be building next door. I recently sold my piece of property because I don't think I'm moving back."

During his dad's playing days, Brandon and the family lived in Lafayette during the winter and in Franklin Lakes, New Jersey, during the season, except for the early days of his dad's career when Ron and Bonnie lived in Queens, New York (the Yankees played the 1974 and 1975 seasons at Shea Stadium in Queens while Yankee Stadium was being renovated). He attended school in Lafayette and after high school went to Millsaps College, a small liberal arts school in Jackson, Mississippi, where he majored in English and minored in theater and classics.

"It's about three hours from Lafayette. It was far enough from home so the parents couldn't just pop in, but close enough to where if I needed to get home quickly, I could."

Brandon was only eight years old when his father retired as a player, but he has memories of going to the ballpark to see the Yankees play.

"Mom took us every time my dad pitched. And even if he wasn't pitching, we would still go. I mean, we wouldn't make every game. I'm sure Mom got annoyed and tired hauling us all over the place. But we would still go. We wouldn't stay for the whole game, or we wouldn't show up right at the beginning, but we'd still go to support the teammates, the families.

"There was a family section, and so all the families sat there, and then the wives and mothers would take us downstairs to the family lounge whenever we started acting up, I guess. And what would happen is that the boys and sometimes the girls, we would all go downstairs and we would play games in the hallways underneath Yankee Stadium until the game ended. And then the boys would go to the locker room with their dads and the girls would go upstairs.

"Playing baseball in the basement of Yankee Stadium was always so much fun. Andre Randolph [Willie's son] and me would go into the clubhouse and get handfuls and handfuls of Bazooka bubble gum. And we'd put it in our pockets and then we'd run outside and give them to our sisters and all the other kids.

"Back in the day, they used to have Yankee family day, which was always fun because the kids would play baseball against their dads. We would all get dressed up in uniforms and your dad would pitch to you. There were people cheering in the stands because it was before a home game. I remember Taylor Mattingly [son of Yankee first baseman Don Mattingly] ran off into right field and was just throwing the ball into the stands. So, Donnie had to go out there and get him."

Sometimes, Brandon would travel to the games with his dad—but not too often, by choice.

"My dad used to like to get to the stadium early, like several hours early, 'cause he had a whole routine that he would do if he was pitching. So, I wasn't going to the stadium and staying there for like seven, eight hours and then the game, you know?"

When Brandon traveled to the ballpark with his dad, the conversation was much like any other father-son talk during a quiet time in the car.

"We never really talked about what he was going to do in the game. And that's just kind of who my dad is. He's not going to be breaking down his strategy of everything. Now, he loves to talk about it, but at the time, it was more like father and son: 'Are you behaving? Your mom said you weren't.'"

In Franklin Lakes, life for Brandon was also much like the life of any young kid growing up in the suburbs.

"Most of our friends were the other ballplayers' kids. That's who becomes your family after a while. The majority of our time, we were hanging out with Willie Randolph [also a Franklin Lakes resident] and his kids because he's got four and we were three, and we're all basically like a year apart in age. There was a brother and sister who lived behind our house that we always hung out with. We lived by the old IBM plant and there was a house that I guess IBM would rent out, so every [summer] we would come back and there was a new family there. So, we would be like, 'Oh, who are the new people?' And we would meet them. And they always had kids, so we always had new friends every summer, at least on one side of our house, which was fun.

"We were just kids. We had a pool, so we would swim. We liked exploring, so we walked through the woods. Dad would hang out with us, jump in the pool with us. We weren't asking, 'Hey, throw me a ball,' you know, if there were times that we would play baseball he would be the pitcher for both teams."

Dad's baseball friends often stopped by the New Jersey house.

"We're southern, so we always liked to have company over and barbecue and grill. Some of the teammates would come over and hang, and the kids would come over. We'd have sleepovers with the kids. Dave Righetti [Yankee pitcher] came over a lot. He was just starting out and my dad had kind of taken him under his wing. This was our life. That's all we knew. Your dad plays baseball, and some guys are going to come over."

Another part of life was being out with Dad in public, which didn't bother Brandon much.

"I didn't feel like I had to share him, and I don't ever remember being upset. I mean, at some points I'm sure that I got annoyed 'cause you're trying to have a conversation and somebody comes up and they're like, 'Hey, can I get an autograph? Can I get a picture?' My dad was never one to turn someone away. The only rule was, if we were all eating as a family and somebody came to the table, he would just ask them to wait until we were done. It was part of my dad's job. The older I got, that's what I realized.

"At probably six or seven years old, you kind of start to figure out that my life wasn't what my friends' lives were. Like, I didn't see my dad for four or five months here and there. But with my mom and my dad, it was never made a big deal. I think, if anything, we were kind of told not to really talk about it, like not really say anything or brag about it because that's just not how my parents raised us. We were not raised to be like, 'Oh, my dad's better than yours because he's a ballplayer.' So, I guess as kids we were just kind of accepting of it. It was just kind of a normal thing for us because we were never told to act like it was a big deal. Other people . . . you have cousins

and aunts and uncles that are like, 'Hey, can you get this?' And I'd be
like, 'I'm seven years old. What am I going to do?' [laughs]. People
would ask me to get my dad's autograph [for them] because they
were scared of him. And I'm like, 'Why? He's not a scary person.
Just go ask him.'"

Back in Lafayette during the winter, things were different.

"It's almost funny because, during the off-season, you didn't have
anyone to talk to about it. You're not hanging out with that baseball
family anymore. I couldn't always explain to my Lafayette friends,
like, 'Oh, I went up to Boston and I did this; I went down to Baltimore and I did this; or we hung out with so-and-so.' First of all,
they didn't care. And second, they didn't understand it. So, it was
just weird."

Wintertime was also a time for his dad to spend with the family.

"It was a lot of catching up. It was always, like, 'How's school going? You guys behaving?' It was a lot of one-on-one time, just seeing
how we were doing and trying to reinsert himself back into our lives.
So, it was always kind of nice when he came home, unless—and I was
famous for doing this because I wasn't the most well-behaved kid—
Mom would sometimes threaten that I would have to wait until my
dad got home before he would give me my punishment. Now, my
dad might not have been coming home for a month. So, she would
be like, 'I told him about it so he's going to have a month to think
of your punishment.' My dad would come home and he'd be like,
'I don't know what you're talking about. Your mom never told me
anything.' My dad would never come home and want to discipline
us because he had been gone for so long. So, when he would come
home it was always like, 'Okay, your mom told me that you got in
trouble, so pretend I'm in here chewing you out.' My dad was never
the disciplinarian. He would never come home and be mad. He
would put baseball aside and become Dad and, you know, hang out,
drop us off at school, which was always fun to him. It was always fun
when he came home."

Brandon didn't particularly enjoy playing baseball, and that was okay with his dad.

"I played Tee-ball and then a few leagues after that, but I wasn't very good. I just wasn't. And I didn't enjoy it. I was a second baseman or an outfielder. But obviously, everybody was like, 'Oh, you're going to pitch. You got that Guidry arm. We're gonna call you Gator Jr., Louisiana Lightning II.' And I was like, 'No.'

"I played until I was probably about nine years old. And then I was like, 'You know what? I don't like this.' Dad was like, that's fine. He never pressured me into playing baseball. He actually told me, don't play baseball. 'Cause he knows what it's like. But I played just to try it out.

"If I actually put my heart and soul into it, it may have been different. But I just didn't enjoy it. I played soccer, I played volleyball. Baseball just wasn't my sport. It just took forever. My mom used to tell me the story. She was like, 'Brandon, you would sit in the outfield and pick flowers. That's how bored you were.' I guess it wasn't exciting for me. Like soccer, you're running around. Volleyball, there's a lot of movement. Baseball was like, 'Okay, I'll sit here.'"

Another of Dad's favorite pursuits that didn't quite enthrall Brandon was duck hunting.

"My dad was, and still is to this day, a big duck hunter. I think I went out on maybe one or two duck hunts with him, but it wasn't my thing. You'd have to get up at like three o'clock in the morning and it's freezing cold. And then you go and sit in the water for hours, just hoping that a duck comes. I remember one time I went I just played with the dog the whole time. The first time I ever had a shot of Wild Turkey was with my dad on the way to a duck hunt because I was freezing and he was like, 'Take a sip of this, it'll warm you up.' It burned so bad and tasted horrible [laughs]. I don't think I ever shot a duck in my life. My dad did not raise a hunter, but he got a hunter in both my brothers-in-law."

Brandon moved to New York when his dad was hired as pitching coach for the Yankees in 2006.

"I always loved the city. My sisters are the country mice and I'm the city mouse. When Dad found out he was going to be the pitching coach, I was like, 'Hey, do you want a roommate?' So, when he moved up here to coach, I moved with him and when he left, I just stayed.

"It was different being a player than being a coach. He would still go to the stadium early, but then he would come home late as well 'cause they would have coaches' meetings. This is when they started using all the cyber metrics, and that wasn't how my dad played and wasn't how he coached, so it was frustrating for him. He's like, okay, but a computer is not going to tell you if [the pitcher] is sick or had a fight with his girlfriend last night. And so, he would stay at the stadium to try to figure things out."

These days, Ron Guidry's primary role is that of grandfather. Brandon is single, but his two sisters have three children and a stepson between them.

"When my niece was born, we tried to get her to call my dad Gator. That's what he wanted. But, for some reason, she got it in her head that it was Coco. So, now that's his name. Everyone calls him Coco except my nephew. He calls him Gator.

"So, my father, the big, tough baseball player, Yankees retired number, captain and all that stuff, he goes by Coco [laughs]. He refers to himself as Coco, too. Like if he's talking to her on the phone, he's like, 'Well, yup, Coco's going to be home.' And it's so funny to me.

"My nieces and nephew, they've got him wrapped around their fingers. Like, my dad bought one of those fun jumps. And it was too hot to play outside so he brought it in the house, in the living room, and moved the furniture. And I was like, 'What's happening to you guys?' We never got to do that. I'm like, 'They're kids, they can be hot' [laughs]. He's so protective and so loving of them. He loves being a grandfather 'cause he gets to spoil them and gets to be with

Brandon Guidry and his dad practice their game faces.
Brandon Guidry

them full-time and watch them grow up. Maybe, in a way, because he didn't get to spend that time with us."

Today, Brandon works for an attorney on real estate and sports marketing, including representing retired athletes like his dad. And Brandon and his dad are regular attendees at the Yankees annual Old Timers' Day festivities.

"It's good because not only is it a reunion for the ballplayers, it is for the families as well. You see people you grew up with, maybe you haven't seen them in some time. We see the [Bobby] Murcer family and the [Thurman] Munson family and the [Catfish] Hunter family, which we were all close to."

The family atmosphere of baseball was important to the Guidrys.

"While [Dad] was taking care of his teammates on the field, [Mom] made sure she was taking care of their families off the field. We all just looked out for each other."

One example occurred in the previously mentioned family lounge.

"There was a glass table, a square table. And so, my mom and one of the other wives were like, 'We can't have this in here with kids.' So, basically, [Mom] and the other wife picked it up, put it in the elevator, hit George Steinbrenner's floor. [Mom] wrote a note. She was like, 'This is Bonnie Guidry. We can't have this in the lounge.' Elevator comes back down, no table. They come back the next day, the whole room had been baby-proofed, like covers on the sockets, no glass table. My mom, if she wanted to, she would get it done."

All in all, Brandon is happy with his childhood as the son of a baseball star.

"I'm perfectly content with the way it was, the positives and the negatives. We had a really nice life. We got to travel, we got to do things that other kids didn't do. I was going to Broadway shows and museums and doing things that I know my friends didn't do. It was fun and it was a learning experience. I never in my life regretted my dad playing baseball. It came with perks, but it came with negativity, too. There was one woman who may or may not have been trying to kidnap me and my sister. You just have weird, random things happen, but I wouldn't trade it, wouldn't change any of it."

A Note on Sources

Statistics and interview leads for this book came from a variety of sources, including *Baseball America 2021 Directory*, LinkedIn, Baseball-Reference.com, Baseball-Almanac.com, the SABR Bio Project, Retrosheet, and the author's own head, which is overstuffed with what until now had been mostly useless baseball stories and facts.

Index

About the Author

Mark Braff retired in November 2020 after more than forty years as a highly regarded public relations professional, the last twenty-seven as a consultant working under the banner of Braff Communications LLC. He resides with his wife in Bergen County, New Jersey.